# Spiritual Famine
# in
# the Age of Plenty

Marlaina Donato

Ekstasis Multimedia

Ekstasis Multimedia: www.booksandbrush.net

Spiritual Famine in the Age of Plenty/Marlaina Donato
Blairstown, New Jersey: Ekstasis Multimedia, LLC, 2013
ISBN-13: 978-0615840826
ISBN-10: 0615840825

Cover art, interior images, & design: Marlaina Donato

For the Self within the self,
in every being.

# Table of Contents

When you drink the water,

remember the spring.

-Chinese Proverb

# Foreword

Humans, like all living creatures on earth, are wired for survival; since the dawn of life, we have spent every minute of our existence hostage to this cellular programming. Progress through the ages has brought much of our world to our present apex of technology and convenience. Most of our mundane comforts were unthinkable to our ancestors, yet our level of discontent in many areas of life has increased.

Generations before us struggled against nature and circumstance, endured back-breaking labor, fell victim to rampant disease, and experienced horrors and loss beyond our modern comprehension, yet the quality of life far exceeded our attempts despite expediency, glossy entertainment, and the razzle-dazzle of 21st Century perks.

*How do you know people in the past had a better quality of life?* you may ask. My answer is simple: culture, art, and community structure do not lie; *the soul of the people* is deeply and unmistakably woven into the literature, art, ethics, and family dynamic of generations past. Many may argue that such observation is born from sentimentality or adherence to outdated societal expectation and ideals, and this very argument, for me, is further evidence of how we have sacrificed meaningfulness on the altar of progress. Human advancement is inevitable, essential, and awe-inspiring, yet progress without evolution of the finer qualities—creativity, ethics, and the integration of flesh, psyche, and primal emotions— can only lead to the extinction of everything that makes us human; it could very well lead to our annihilation, period.

It is becoming increasingly obvious how we've become dependent upon constant distraction, instant gratification, and mostly, escape. We live in a culture where we are so uncomfortable with our own lives and emotions that we run for a drink, pop a pill, shoot up, stuff our bellies, shop ourselves into monumental debt, have Band-Aid sex, saturate ourselves with Hollywood superficiality, overbook our schedules and overwork our bodies until exhaustion and lose ourselves in the attempt to numb what comes with being human. Life and its totality includes the difficult and sometimes agonizing emotional terrain of deep grief, loneliness, anxiety, self-doubt, frustration, devastating loss, failure, illness, psychological scars, unrequited love, rage, disappointment, and generational dysfunction.

What if we raised our children to reach for something outside of themselves that brings them healing, creative expression, upliftment, and transformation? What if we pursued our hunger for beauty, community, wholeness, health, and freedom instead of simply filling the empty pit? What if we redefined our priorities so we could have time to commune with nature, pick up a brush, learn an instrument, cook a meal, take a class, or say a prayer? What would happen if we dared to change our definition of happiness and realize that having ourselves is far more important than having everything? In the end, isn't that *everything?*

Gone are the days when we actually acknowledged each other at the market or had face-to-face conversations on a regular basis; gone are children who are capable of going through a few hours or a full day without constant entertainment that impairs their ability to interact with people and the world around them.

I know I am not alone when I say that I struggle as a human being in these times. I have seen human kindness and common decency dwindle to a spark; I have seen the family unit splinter into new definitions that rarely include a two-parent household or at the least, a common meal; I have seen children descend into physical and mental sickness; I have seen our culture explode into a medication-dependent society and the medical establishment into a robotic, greed-fueled institution; I have seen women who wanted it all and ended up with miserable kids, broken relationships, and heart disease; I have seen our once-thriving country crumble where abandoned houses become part of the landscape; I have seen our government decay into an entity that has no respect for human life, rights, or integrity; I have seen my most trusted relationships rot in the names of pseudo reasons such as Too Busy.

Yeah, we're all busy—busy running a million miles

standing still and having very little happiness to show for it.

What if each of us sat with our own demons and truly faced them? What if we saw pain as normal instead of a symptom? What if The Answer is simply accepting that sometimes, there is no answer? What if... What a beautiful possibility.

Technology and modern convenience enables us to live and survive better in many ways, but it is too easy to allow it to enslave our humanity and capability of nourishing what means the most in our lives. Some of us shut our eyes to the reality of things—sometimes we must shut our eyes to maintain sanity and health, but sometimes we also have to look at it dead-on and acknowledge what is. It might offend a lot of people; it might put us in a tail-spin of depression; it might brand us politically incorrect and "uncool"; we might be seen as crazy if we choose a quieter, simpler path; it might murder some defiant ideals along the way. But it can also set us free, and freedom—on all levels—is worth it.

Yes, we can change the world, not in the way we were led to believe, but by simply changing our own lives. Perhaps, it is possible that we will someday see our reflections and see our unfathomable beauty and be inspired to live it without question and without boundary. This book is not about bashing technology or our modern achievements; it is not suggesting that we form off-the-grid existences and meditate our days away; rather, it is an invitation...

I invite you to answer your innermost hunger for more—more time, more inner peace, more passion, more contentment, more of *you* in your own life, more reasons for living. If this book is in your hands, you have been called to change your life on the *minute* level in exchange for significant transformation. It doesn't take money, quitting your job, or following a guru. It only takes willingness to see things in a different light. We can't change the world, but we can change our corner of it. Come on, let's see how wonderful and beautiful we can make it.

# Part I

## A Million Miles Standing Still

# 1

# The Quest for Everything

## Addiction to Activity

In the modern American world, work rarely concludes at day's end but continues in a different form the moment one steps through the door. Weekends and holidays are jam-packed and scheduled; even vacations leave us with little breathing room, each moment booked as if relaxing means we are missing out on something—or worse—we are "doing nothing." How many times have you spent time away and then returned home and felt like you needed a vacation from the vacation?

In our fast-paced world, being a parent or caregiver, paying the bills, and sometimes basic survival can automatically nominate us for the Atlas role, balancing the world on our shoulders; there is little time for a lunch break much less feeding our deepest soul-level needs. Many times our spirits starve, so we add yet even more responsibility to our shoulders in some vain attempt to compensate for our feeling of lack. A lot of us slip into the habit of wearing our obligations like a badge of honor. "I'm a good mother," is often heard when we ask a woman about the last time she sat down or did something for her own wellbeing. "If I didn't do what I do, everything and everyone would fall apart!" is another common response. Until the day comes when that eight-armed Hindu goddess of Doing Everything buckles under the weight of sudden illness, fatigue, depression, or addiction; worse, when that woman comes to the end of her life realizing that she had a spotless house, transported the kids to every single game and music lesson and never said the word "no" yet couldn't remember more than a handful of times when she actually enjoyed any of it.

Past generations struggled through life growing, hunting, preserving, and cooking every morsel of food that went into their mouths and the mouths of their growing children; keeping house meant fetching water from an outdoor source by pail and bucket, doing laundry on wash boards for sometimes enormous families, making candles for light on dark nights, tending hearth fires for cooking and for warmth, making and mending clothing, and taking care of livestock on which they were dependent for food, transportation, and labor. Yet stories and memories were passed down, the harvest celebrated, milestones and passages honored, and time for rest and reflection observed.

Fast forward to 21$^{st}$ Century America. We get into our cars and travel a block or a few miles to the nearest supermarket (some open 24/7) where we have a world of sustenance at our fingertips: canned, frozen, packaged, boxed, sliced, chopped and diced, already-cooked-broiled-boiled-fried-sautéed-sauced,domestic, imported, staple food, junk food, fast food, ethnic, exotic, gourmet, special diet, and anything imaginable is at our disposal—from the simple to the sometimes ridiculously superfluous. We pick out new clothing at the mall, create light with the flick of a switch, click the remote to choose from hundreds of channels for a variety of entertainment, select the fifteen-minute speed wash on our washing machines, and pop the dishes into the dish washer; yet we cannot find the time to notice a sunset even when we're trapped in dead-stop commuter traffic on the way home from work because we're most likely busy gabbing away on our cell phones about nothing we will remember ten minutes from now. Even when we're lying in bed at night, The To-Do List circles in our brains like an obnoxious, annoying fly incapable of leaving us alone.

When we compare the list of obligations to the life-depending responsibilities of generations past, we come up short in the priority department yet cannot fathom eliminating one thing from The List. Activity can become an addiction; it can destroy our cherished relationships, compromise our health, and steal our ability to be in our own lives.

## Emotional Anesthesia

In the daily chaos, we often do not take time to even acknowledge our own emotions and get in the insidious habit of stuffing whatever comes up, be it sadness, frustration, grief, anger, or depression. When we ignore feelings, they tend to build up from the cellular level and resurface as the need for more distraction so we don't have to face the underlining issue. Little by little, the spare moments of our lives get eaten up by saying "yes" to yet another commitment, running more errands than necessary, taking on more projects at work, finding more ways to entertain the kids, adding on more home improvement plans, and anything else that might prevent us from feeling what we do not want to feel. People around us get used to the Atlas façade and make us feel guilty if we hint at saying "no." No one wants to be labeled *a bad parent, a negligent wife, a community slacker,* or *uncaring friend.* But the reality is this: yes, we can do it all and have it all, but not without a price. And that price is most often our truest selves.

Attempting to numb pressurized emotion may give us the illusion that we are stronger than our problems and immune to vulnerability. The compulsion puts us on a wheel of chaos, and doing becomes our drug of choice, failing to realize that days, weeks, months, and even years can go by before we actually *feel* something. Often, we end up having an unprecedented meltdown, after which, we dust ourselves off and begin the numbing process all over again.

## Constant Contact, Little Communication

Our ancestors did not have the luxury of instant communication with loved ones; letters could take weeks or months to reach their destination, and visits were often impossible due to distance and obligations to mere survival. Sometimes parents never saw their grown children again if they moved out of the area, and certainly, never even met their own grandchildren. Today, we can go online and read an email or pop onto a social media site to see the latest pictures and videos of first smiles and first steps, weddings, and birthdays. Some of us take our cell phones into the bathroom with us so we don't miss any calls or texts. We are in an age of constant contact, not only with loved ones but people and friends from childhood whom we haven't seen in thirty, forty, even fifty years. We keep tabs on what they have for dinner, where they go on vacation, and what they wore to a party the previous weekend, yet we rarely have true conversation. The word *conversation* is defined as informal, "a talk with somebody about *opinions, ideas, feelings*, or everyday matters." (emphasis mine) Yes, we talk on that cell phone a lot, but how often can we say that our exchange actually includes opinions, ideas and feelings?

The art of conversation is dying; our young people often find it painful to speak to others, and I see this even among adults. Even if we get the ball rolling with a mundane question, the effort to respond can be awkward and devoid of encouragement to go any further. When did the spoken word become such a chore? When did a friendly word to a stranger at the market become something to shun? Words are energy; they have great power to create or destroy, and perhaps, withholding them can be destructive beyond our imagining. As a society, we are no longer willing to share our opinions, ideas, and feelings because much of the time, we program ourselves to turn them off so we can focus on the most important thing: The To-Do List.

## Whose Life are you Living?

Every spring, in my corner of the world, barely-noticeable snippets of life transform into ambitious tufts of green until the woods are dappled with every imaginable hue: sage, chartreuse, jade, emerald, olive, hazel, even a hint of teal if the light is coming through at a certain angle toward the end of the day. For one glorious month, we see the trees unfurl their uniqueness, each daring to stand in the light expressing its unique shade of green before summer comes in with an unseen hand and smudges the colors into one indiscernible tone. Each year I witness the magic descend into the inevitable blending-in, and I cannot help but conclude that humans are very similar to the trees.

We come on the scene boisterous and delighted, unapologetic about being one-of-a-kind; unaware of outside prejudice and preferences, we live and breathe in a state of perfect authenticity and diversity. Somewhere along the line, not long into childhood, we begin the process of homogenization. Blame it on nature or nurture, too many of us conform to the unspoken obligation to be part of the "norm"—or whatever definition of that is acceptable at the time.

What choices would you make differently if you truly lived *your* life, not the one you *think* you should be living? Whose life are you really living?

## Acquisition: The Next Mirage

From the moment we begin our first steps, we are presented with a life agenda dictated by society that usually goes something like this: go to school; graduate; go to another school and sometimes another for that degree; rake in a good salary; meet a life partner and settle down; buy a house; have a family; pay the bills; give your kids everything you didn't have and a hundred times more; pay off the mortgage; retire; have your finances in order and pre-pay your own funeral arrangements; leave something behind for your loved ones; go to Heaven. And then there's the fine print: *Snuff out all creative instincts; it's not practical. Choose a career that will pay well not necessarily make you happy. Live in a certain kind of house and drive a certain kind of car or you will be considered a failure. Look cool at all costs. Go into debt following trends because anything is better than not keeping up with the Joneses. Listen to authority, even if your heart and your gut tell you something's wrong. Keep your true feelings to yourself; don't rock the boat. Smile and say "everything's fine" because admitting that it's not is somehow a shortcoming. Look as young as possible for as long as possible. Believe in your parents' religion because you've been told to do so and even if your heart is leading you on another path, stick with the set path just in case. Give up your interests, passions, and hobbies to foster your kids' interests, passions, and hobbies. Brand anyone not living according to The Agenda as an impractical outsider.* Most of us get halfway through our lives and realize that The Agenda isn't what it's cracked up to be and there just might be a Plan B or C or D. Most of us feel old before our time trying to adhere to the expectations of our culture, and mostly, ourselves. Our quest to be part of the norm can kill individuality, originality, inner peace, and spiritual autonomy. In simple terms, the true self is lost even before it is found.

Every day we are bombarded with the latest and hottest trends in technology, fashion, food, entertainment, and health, and we put *Gotta Get It* on The To-Do List. Most of the time, Gotta Get It makes us deliriously happy and makes all that overtime and missed vacations and days off worth every penny toward The Thing that makes us momentarily content, The Thing that lifts our spirits, The Thing that makes life easier, The Thing everyone else has, The Thing our kids want because their friends have It, The Thing that is always replaced with Another Thing. The only problem is the subsequent domino effect.

People who travel to Third World countries will often marvel at the level of happiness of those they come in contact with—children with no running water, families with very little food, and communities enduring squalid conditions compared to our mainstream American life. Happiness in the presence of horrible suffering and lack is something to be envied, and it can make us question the very meaning of the word *happiness*. We each have our own idea of it, our hopes for it, and make it our life's quest. Sometimes the definition of it is someone else's; we try it on for size, and even if it doesn't quite fit who we are, go after it anyway because it seems like the logical, socially-correct thing to do.

Happiness is a fleeting emotion, yet the very idea of it is something most of us strive to have every day of our lives. What would happen if we turned the coin over and found contentment? Contentment is more of a long-term possibility and goes much deeper than happiness; perhaps we have been conditioned to believe that they are one and the same, when in reality, they are very different.

Happiness is an endorphin rush, that jump-out-of-your-skin glee that comes with passing gains, events, and infatuation; it is impossible to sustain. And that is the hook: find something that can keep that euphoria in motion. Unfortunately, happiness is a spinning top that cannot rotate infinitely, and we can exhaust ourselves and even become addicted in the search. On the other hand, contentment is a state of being that does not waver despite life's fluctuations; it is not elation that comes with a price tag of the inevitable crash but a sustained harmony at the core of even the most challenging days. Contentment is what we envy most in our pets, that state of Now that does not obsess about the past or future and never grows tired of the common and the everyday.

Often, contentment springs from a beautiful attribute called thanksgiving. Gratitude, even a speck, can be a jewel in the muck of life. The most thankful people are most often the most fulfilled, and their inner harmony depends little on acquirements or social status.

Living, during any century, is arduous and exhausting. It is human to seek out balm, momentary or permanent, that makes it all tolerable, all worthwhile. Acquisition, be it material or emotional, professional or personal, shimmers on the horizon, promising satiety and benediction. The promise of oasis is powerful and believable, and there isn't a human being on the planet who has escaped the need for it. Sometimes the mirage is so vivid and realistic that we look at other people who appear to have found Eldorado with envy, comparing ourselves and our circumstances, not knowing that the ones we envy may be envying us for the same reasons.

## Voluntary Imprisonment

Imprisoning ourselves happens over the course of many years without our realizing and is often attributed to necessity; survival programs us, self-image compels us. Many people find success in the worldly sense, yet contentment eludes them. Perhaps, for long-term wellbeing and possibility of contentment, we must learn—even force ourselves—to redefine success. Finding new meaning of the word does not require settling for or being less, but quite the opposite—to challenge our self-imposed boundaries and feel that we are worth more than settling for a life that is contrary to our own nature and what we are truly capable of.

How many of us crucify ourselves in the name of Not Good Enough? How many of us end up siding with our critics, naysayers, envious peers, and indifferent loved ones? Our brains replay tapes from the past until we recite them from the cellular level. How many times do we relinquish our deepest selves because the world might judge us? The world? The world is not hateful strangers, indifferent family, or critical friends but after all is said and done, *our own consciousness*. We cannot change people or how they react to our God-given right to live and love by our own accord, but we can change our consciousness. So simple, so incredibly difficult. But doable. Albert H. Davis says, "Freedom is having nothing to prove." It is a beautiful truth, one that demands the courage to redefine words and concepts that form the very foundation of our culture.

Each of us is born with the right to be who we are—and over the course of a lifetime, that could mean many different selves; each human being has a spiritual DNA and a duty to honor and nourish that unique soul-print. Yet we humans get caught on the wheel of judgment and self-judgment. How many choices end up bad ones because we put too much value on how we are seen to loved ones and strangers alike? Addiction, eating disorders, discontent, self-hatred, relationship and career decisions, where we live, what we drive, what we wear, and how we live can all be somehow traced back to—or tainted by—the feeling that there is something to prove.

## Postponing Joy

Through life's journey, the mirage in the distance can affect how, and if, we respond to the positive things in our lives. "I'll be happy when I pay off the loan," or "I'll be happy when I go on vacation," or "I'll worry about my own happiness after the kids are grown and on their way," or "I'll be happy after I sign that contract," are common ways of thinking, and years can go by without us realizing that because of this conditional deal with outcome, we can miss out on moments of deep joy and beauty.

Postponing joy is usually a sign that we are dependent upon getting what we need or want in order to allow room for enjoyment, as if we need something else to happen before we give ourselves permission to truly live. Sometimes we cannot find enjoyment while our loved ones are struggling or are unhappy in life, as if stifling our own pleasure somehow benefits them. There may also be the subconscious and sometimes-conscious belief that we must earn joy. Self-deprivation is not beneficial or virtuous—whether it is well-intended out of empathy for another person or waiting for That Something to happen for ourselves. Postponing joy is self-destructive and sets us up for cynicism and burnout. Most of all, it is an indication that we have put ourselves last in our own lives. And we deserve much more than that.

## Estrangement from Self

Have you ever been too busy to notice how you feel physically? A slight sore throat? Chronic indigestion? Too busy to notice your emotions? Depressed, angry, sad? Have you been too busy to feel much of anything? Estrangement from ourselves is inevitable with jam-packed lives. "If I cry, I'll never stop," or "If I stopped to notice every ache and pain, nothing would ever get done," we might say, putting more importance on the objective. For many of us, acknowledging our physical complaints or emotional climate feels self-indulgent in the face of what needs to be accomplished by the end of any given day. We have been conditioned to believe that our emotional and spiritual lives are secondary to our obligations and responsibilities, even if that means dying a little inside more each day.

Unfortunately, separating our emotional and spiritual selves from our physical selves has a dangerous side effect: we can get so accustomed to turning off how we feel, we can also lose the ability to listen to our own bodies which might have severe consequences to the whole self.

The whole self. Those involved in the holistic arts see each person as a trinity of being- body, mind, and spirit; this philosophy is an ancient one, something we have tragically lost along the way. In tribal cultures, this splintering of self is sometimes call soul loss. In the spiritual sense, soul loss can occur from trauma, buried or remembered, and pieces of ourselves leave the whole. We can go years feeling that something is missing, and that something can very well be a vital part of our essence, the part that enables us to be awake in our own lives, to relish the positive and the joyful, to experience the depths of our own existence.

Belief in the tribal definition of soul loss is not a prerequisite to feel that something inside of us has been lost along the way. Trauma does not have to be born from tragedy, illness, or abuse but anything that changes us, from one consciousness into another. Perhaps, adapting to "the real world" and burying our true selves and dreams that seem impractical is traumatic enough for soul loss. Our passage into adulthood includes conformance; dreams of the faithful and hopeful child-self die and are replaced with pragmatic objectives, goals that will ensure our security in life. I wonder what would happen if we also included the security of our other selves in this equation? Security of body, mind, and spirit is a foreign concept in a one dimensional, goal-driven society, but it is one that deserves contemplation and invitation.

# 2

# Soul Hunger

## Alienation from Nature

The larger our world becomes, lives become busier and the natural world beyond the window seems to get further away. When we are children, we are more inclined to get a breath of fresh air, walk the dog in the park, spend a day on the water, or dip our toes in a brook. As we get older, days get shorter with responsibilities; many of us come home when it is dark and that chance to get a ray or two of sunlight becomes almost impossible. Sometimes our lives are so overflowing with obligation that we can forget there is a natural world outside of the chaos. The less time we spend in nature, the more likely we are to disregard it altogether.

Our polluted and depleted natural resources indicate how we have forgotten the part we play in the whole—that what affects an ocean across the world will eventually affect us. Many of us in the Western world often feel untouchable; our level of convenience has enabled us to live independently and unlike our ancestors, have no need to rely on our neighbors for survival. Unfortunately, our wonderful age of progress and autonomy has forged a chasm between individual and community, and most of all, between individual and nature. We no longer need to tend to gardens and field crops for our own food consumption. Our direct dependence upon and our interaction with the natural world has been replaced with dependence upon commercial production. When we go to the local supermarket and pick out vegetables or choose a steak for dinner, we fail to make the connection between the land and our bellies, between farmer and table. In ancient times and in the not too-distant past, our relationship with the soil, seasons, and weather enabled us to realize our place in the whole, to co-exist with the natural rhythms of life; our ancestors could taste the rain and the sun in the food they ate, for every single morsel was brought to fruition by a collaborative effort between individual and organic environment. Though, most of us have the luxury of not having to grow or hunt for our sustenance, we are also deprived of this fusion of energies. The circle has been broken, and despite the fact that this is not considered to be a contributing factor in our declining health, who's to say we are not affected? Take any living creature or plant, for example, and see what happens when it is removed from its natural habitat. Failure to thrive and death are inevitable.

We humans are the most complex beings on planet Earth, and looking through holistic eyes, our loss of habitat (direct interaction with natural cycles) makes me wonder if many of our ills are rooted in this alienation from Gaia. Add genetically modified foods, chemicals that kill nutrients in the soil—along with pests and fungus, and artificial ingredients to cut costs and prolong shelf life—and we have even less of what nature intends for our innate human constitution.

Due to our modern varied lifestyles and living conditions, and individual circumstances and limitations, it is not plausible to suggest that we return to the laborious existence of our ancestors (very few of us would want to) yet small and simple additions to our daily lives could mend the chasm just a bit. And just a bit could go a long way.

Studies show that hospital patients in rooms with windows overlooking some kind of green recover more quickly and have less pain. The sight, sound, and smells of the natural world have remarkable effects on our immune systems and psyches. Could not many of us who work in offices also benefit? Would it be too far-fetched or poetic to suggest that cubicle employees, retail workers, and students include something in their environment to bring the outside in? A living plant or two on a desk. A photograph of a waterfall, meadow, or ocean near the computer. A drop of lavender or spruce essential oil on a tissue to inhale during a long business meeting or school day. Finding a patch of grass during a lunch break. A beautiful rock or river stone used as a paper weight. Nature recordings on our iPods while we take the subway. Just a few possibilities to bring some green into the daily gray.

There seems to be too little time in the day for depth,

including the simple *deep* breath. Strip mall parking lots are often landscaped with trees and shrubbery, an unlikely invitation during our hectic days to take a few minutes to notice the colors and changing seasons; two minutes reserved to simply stand beneath a young gingko or oak and admire its parasol of leaves blowing in the wind can boost our neurotransmitters and lower blood pressure. Not unlike the legendary prayer flags of Tibet, each leaf, for us, can also become consecrated as the wind takes our hearts' unuttered worries.

Recently, on my way through a parking lot, I noticed tiny flowers the size of the head of a pin. I knelt down to touch their miniscule blue faces, and others, slightly larger, with pansy-like purple smiles. I marveled at tiny petals undisturbed from my heavy step as they sprang back with gentle defiance. "I am here," they seemed to say, "invisible to most, but here." The tiniest flowers of the field reminded me that each of us matters. Sometimes wisdom comes in the size of a pin, a speck of joy when we need it most.

May we all be like the forgotten flowers, growing beside oaks with the same intention, passion, and willingness to have faith in our own presence in an overwhelming world.

## Emotion as Cultural Enemy

Of course, I could tell very few people about those tiny flowers that had a message for me that day; finding such meaning in the natural world in the 21$^{st}$ Century might be considered a little silly and worse, sentimental. Yet, the word itself, defined by my dictionary at hand, includes: *refined or tender emotion; manifestation of the higher or more refined feelings.* It is interesting to see this meaning compared to the synonyms: *gushy, syrupy, romantic, maudlin, emotional.*

Emotional. It is an adjective that can suggest weakness, instability, and unprofessionalism. In our male-dominant culture, it can also connote femininity (subconscious) and the right side of the brain—in other words, antithesis of all things logical (conscious) and intellectually valid.

We are thrust into professional arenas where it is very clear that emotional response is not allowed, tolerated, or endorsed. The moment we step into our jobs and careers, we are expected—and expect ourselves—to proceed without feeling or risk losing respect and position, if not employment. Even practitioners in the holistic arts, especially therapeutic massage therapists, are considered to violate ethical boundaries if empathy is expressed verbally or with a touch on the shoulder.

In the realm of entertainment, films from the '30s, '40s, '50s, '60s, and '70s often had strong emotional themes portraying human relationships that offered inspiration and something to feel good about when we walked out of the theater. Today these films are regarded as sentimental, idealistic, and of lesser value when compared to present day action-packed, noise-filled, and edgy productions; we rarely leave a movie theater feeling uplifted or hopeful. Anything with deep-felt positivity is labeled as corny and is usually panned by the critics.

Professional restraint, slick entertainment, and media opinion directly oppose human emotional response; the overall message of our century is to emulate our technology—efficient and lifeless; when we compound this with busy lives that do not allow time for connection to feelings, is it any wonder why we are experiencing an epidemic of numbness and apathy? Somewhere along the way, we bought into the idea that to possess genuine emotions is something to hide and be ashamed of. Our innate human faculties have become the enemy within, fires that need to be smothered. We are in a new age of progress, and anyone who dares to bring a laugh into the boardroom, a childish hope in the face of reality or an honest answer when it would be more fashionable to put on airs is seen as sentimental, or naive–in other words, too *human*, and this alone makes me very concerned about the human race. How many of us resort to self-monitoring and the word "too" cluttering up our inner dialogue? How many times a day? A week? A month? A year? A lifetime? Answer: *too* damn much.

Flip over reservation, emotionlessness, and detachment and we find rampant anger, the only emotion that seems to see the light of day; it's on the highway, on the long line at the grocery store, in the classroom, and on the Internet. Expression of rage over sometimes-petty incidents seems to be steam blowing off a very large pressure cooker. We may be numb and disconnected but boiling beneath the surface.

## Pain as Ally

The biological intention of pain is to alert us when something in our bodies is compromised. Its main objective is to prevent further injury or loss of energy in order for the healing process to happen. Emotional pain, in my opinion, is powered by the same innate wisdom to bring us back to a state of equilibrium. It is also human, especially in today's times, to want to shoot the messenger—pop a pill, down a drink, overeat, and pursue risky activities and relationships just to name a few, in attempt to cover up the pain. But what if we started seeing our emotions as allies instead of adversaries and allowed them to tell us what we need to change in our lives? What would happen if we looked at pain as an ally? Circumstantial depression, emotional fatigue, anxiety, sadness, emptiness, and anger as teachers trying to show us what we need to change in our lives, perhaps in ourselves?

## Fast Food Relationships

In the rush of life, it is difficult to find cohesive—the wonderful bonds between us that seem to be more challenged than any other time in history. Face-to-face relationship has been replaced with instant forms of communication; texting, an abbreviated version of the already-instantaneous email, is often the preferred means of dialogue because it simply takes less time.

It is common to see friendships dwindle down to a passing comment on social media sites. Skimming the surface of our daily lives can be squeezed onto The To-Do List and often avoids accessing what lies beneath—or in other words, anything emotional which requires more time, something few of us have. If it can be managed, we have coffee with a friend or delight in each other's presence for a few minutes as we pass by on the way to our next appointment.

After a while, if we are paying attention, we realize how superficial our alliances have become. Meaning in relationships can seem like a luxury, and luxury is not pragmatic. Some of us resign ourselves to the fact that this is the name of the game in the modern era, and true friendship will withstand the new rules. Yes, friendships based upon external experience—people, places, and things—will most certainly survive because they need very little nourishment to survive. On the other hand, relationships based upon depth, shared emotional experience, and spiritual and intellectual kinship are like gardens; if they are not tended to, the weeds take over and strangle growth. Anyone with a garden wouldn't dream of neglecting it by withholding water, light, and nourishment; the consequences are obvious. Human relationships—the ones rooted in deep soil—also die without responsiveness and care.

We are in the age of fast food relationships because it has become too easy to neglect each other in the name of Busy. There is an unspoken expectation to be pardoned because of the B word, and any of us who do not want to settle for this is seen as overly sensitive or more often, insensitive to our loved ones lost in the whirlwind of the modern world. After all is said and done, true human depth and beauty of exchange is sacrificed, leaving us isolated. Emotional inaccessibility is one of the saddest and unnecessary states of the modern individual, and it can destroy the most beautiful alliances, even within families.

Cultivating substance does not require hours of time, money, or sacrificing something on The To-Do List; it only takes the wisdom to know that at the journey's end, nothing on that list will be remembered except the relationships we did not allow to become casualties in the survival game.

## The Hunger to be Heard

Each bird in the wild has a song, each tree a different expression of leaf, each animal a defense mechanism. It is easy to see how nature groups itself into kindred communities—plants, trees, animals, insects; even certain minerals such as malachite and azurite exist together by higher design. The wild, purple phlox thrives near the tall and unassuming white-flowered garlic mustard; ground ivy fares well near the violet; totter grass blows in the wind, brushing against humble buttercups.

We humans are an odd lot, blooming where we're planted but often finding roots in many soils throughout a lifetime. Our kindred circles form and collapse then form again with a different set of characters. We are fortunate if we find one or two fellow humans with whom to weather our seasons. The soul's search to glimpse itself in another or to be understood is a human longing that transcends culture and time. This sometimes-agonizing quest begins in our own family dynamic, and we wonder where—and if—our true tribe exists. It can continue through love unions, friendships, work relationships; we find ourselves confused and guilty when even our closest loved ones cannot feel the pulse of our deepest passions and personal, unique struggles. In a world of incomprehensible suffering, the need for visibility and spiritual understanding can feel self-indulgent until we remember nature's infinite order. Foxes do not live with coyotes; birds do not live with rabbits. The wild rose does not bloom with poppies.

We, too, need life-nourishing community, spirits who need the same kind of soil, the same certain angle of sunlight, the same amount of rain, the same kind of tending-to. There are many different species of human beings, and it is our inborn right to seek those who harmonize with our truest essence.

Sacred circles are possible. Sacred community is a human need, not a luxury. Sacred non-blood families converge not a moment before we are ready. The sacred is alive and well, even in these challenging and often dark times. If we leave our hearts ajar. If we know we are deserving. If we refuse to put down roots in toxic soil and settle for less.

Once, my husband and I were driving to the market and noticed a bank on the right, one we hadn't noticed before. It turned out that the bank had been there for years, yet neither one of us ever took note of it halfway into the twelve-mile trip between our house and the supermarket. We looked at each other in amazement and then started laughing.

Buildings are not the only thing human beings miss along the journey of our days; we also miss things much closer to home, including people. How many times we have noticed something about a loved one we had never seen over the course of years or decades; it is always a pleasant surprise when the blinders come off and we find something that lights up our hearts and we wonder why it took us so long to actually see.

Artists nourish the ability to look beneath the surface, beneath the top light right into the depth of shadow where true essence lies. Still life, landscape, or lifescape—all things possess dimension, and it is very sad that we humans most often settle for the shiny exterior before we make definitive conclusions about situations and people. The result is a feeling of invisibility and separation; those who mean the most to us do not (and sometimes will not) meet our authentic selves eye to eye. Perhaps one of the greatest fears in the human heart is that we leave this earth without truly being known. Perhaps we should take more responsibility for this and allow others to see the extent of our be-ing, to know it's okay and our birthright.

A little over a year ago, I received an unexpected card in the mail from a dear friend. "I see you," she wrote, little else. The power and simplicity of those three words struck my heart like an anvil of light validating the shadows. Someone had actually parted the branches to find the fruit, and it was a defining moment.

What would happen if we all turned to a loved one today and said, "I see you...?" It might change a life, even our own.

# 3
# The Luxury of Wellbeing

## Rest, a Four Letter Word

Busy people have always struggled to find more time for leisure and recuperation, but as recently as a few generations ago, Sunday was observed as the day of rest, substantial family time which included a special dinner, and taking a break from the strains of life. Today, for most, the entire weekend is considered "down time" yet we manage to jam-pack our days off even more than weekdays. Our children's and grandchildren's sports and other activities, shopping, catching up on housework, and a million other things steal the weekend right out from under us, and before we know it, Monday morning rolls around and we are more exhausted than ever.

The modern human being has become a creature reluctant to say "no" to anyone and anything, one that takes great pleasure in being a people pleaser and putting self last on the list, if at all. Books and magazines we want to read pile up; taking a walk by the water or sitting under the tree out back with a glass of iced tea becomes the plan we never quite get to; soaking in a tub to ease our tired muscles becomes a fantasy. Monotony weighs on our morale as the constant pace takes its toll on our bodies. Not eating on the run, eating better food, getting more exercise, receiving massage and other bodywork, meditating, sleeping in, taking a half-hour nap, and unplugging from the world seems like Science Fiction in probability. Physical and mental balance and vitality are fundamental to life, and all of these things improve state of health yet most of them are noticeably absent on the agenda. Somewhere along the line, wellbeing became a forbidden luxury, and our physical bodies are paying for it. We feel old before our time and suffer Monday morning blues every day of the week. Many of us book salon appointments and make time to shop at department stores yet fail to consider our health. Even self-proclaimed fitness and health advocates fail to realize that health is a trinity: body, mind, and spirit, and all the supplements in the world cannot replace lost sleep, mental rest, and emotional discernment.

Sometimes going shopping is seen as a recreational activity, a form of mental relaxation. Spending can give us joy in the moment and a boost of dopamine that floods us with false energy. But what we need most is a word that has become a no-no in our culture. R-E-S-T. **R**elax. **E**xhale. **S**top. **T**hrive.

## Guilt for Not Doing

As young children, most of us can remember having the glorious ability to do absolutely nothing of significance. As a kid, I loved to skip rocks and throw stones into still water so I could count the circles rippling beyond my field of vision. I especially enjoyed it when there was an extraordinary patch of sky reflected in the lake, and liquid clouds—shocked by sunlight—melted into cream when my rock broke the surface. As an adult, the urge to do this still crosses my mind, but I find myself reluctant to follow the desire, as if play is somehow valueless. During these times I mourn my child-self, the self that could have fun without guilt and tell seriousness to take a hike.

Somewhere in our past, someone in authority—be it a parent, teacher, coach, or family member—planted a tiny seed in our brains that programmed us to believe that somehow we must earn our existence. We became self-conscious, self-critical perfectionists who equate leisure, self-care, and be-ing with laziness and wasting precious time. *Idle hands are the Devil's playthings. Keep busy. Look alive. Get off your duff. Don't be a slacker. Idleness is the beginning of all vices.* Each of us has heard these expressions or others like them at one time or another, and at one point, began to repeat them to ourselves when the mere thought of doing nothing enters our consciousness. If we manage to ignore the societal guilt trip, we find it almost impossible to relax and enjoy doing nothing without the nagging feeling that we could be doing something more constructive. The Yiddish proverb, *the hardest work is to go idle* rings truer than ever.

## Noise

Five-hundred channels or more are available on the

average television, yet there is rarely anything worth the time we spend flipping through them or tolerating the barrage of pharmaceutical, liquor, and often-mindless entertainment commercials. The noise levels of the advertisements send us scrambling to find the mute button. The constant noise on the TV, in the movie theater, and on the radio has increased considerably with each decade. Even the once-silent environment of libraries has been marred with unexplained tolerance of loud cell phone conversations and kids on computers. Cities are getting louder, and suburbs are getting busier and more congested. To add to the noise, during the summer and fall, the ritual of lawn-cutting and leaf-clearing gets in the mix—mowers, leaf blowers, and trimmers howling, growling, and buzzing, sometimes even in the rain. In the winter months, the nasal whine of snow blowers fills any given neighborhood. Go to the supermarket, and by the time we get to the dairy aisle, it is possible to overhear four cell phone conversations and everyone within ten feet knows as much as the person on the other end of the phone.

Many of us get so accustomed to noise, that removing it can be problematic and even anxiety-provoking. Sometimes the distraction of noise helps us cope with life's transitions through grief, living alone, illness, and the fear of death, and some of us can only get to sleep with the backdrop of the television, radio, or white noise machine. Noise is a double-edged sword—one that is both bane and balm.

In short, it seems almost un-American if we do not want and demand *more*, *louder*, and *bigger*. With so much external noise surrounding us, there is very little room for internal silence. Through the ages, anyone with a desire for inner peace sought refuge in retreat, religious community, vision quest, and the heart of nature where noise does not compete with the internal landscape. Environmental noise in conjunction with inner noise (our thoughts, fears, worries, hurts, The to-Do List) is a recipe for unrest, even when we purposely seek out silence and peace. We try to sit in meditation or lie in bed to get a good night's rest, but the noise continues with the human tendency to analyze and fix our problems. Most of us wish there was an Off button somewhere in our brains; between nature's programming and culture's nurturing, we are between a rock and a hard place.

## Loss of the Senses

In the whirlwind of the everyday, our ability to be observant, to listen, to taste, to feel, and to smell can be dulled. That burning mural of sunset ahead of us on the highway might as well be invisible as we make our way home from work, or that gourmet meal at a five-star restaurant could leave us flat; a beautiful song on the radio or the loud crash of something falling nearby might go unnoticed, or the scent of our neighbor's flower garden eludes our nostrils. That soft touch of spring rain on our skin fails to light up the pleasure centers of our brains. Raising a family, sustaining a career, maintaining a marriage, and simply living can take out the highs and lows of life, including sensual responses that were much more intense when were younger and more care-free. Sometimes it takes a lot more of something to affect or impress us. That feel-good dopamine rush from something sweet, a new love affair, a glass of wine, or a rock concert becomes harder to come by, and we seek out more to get that feeling of being alive. In the process, we can become jaded and flat-lined; life becomes a faded photograph, its once-vibrant colors and nuances lost.

Perhaps, during this earthly journey, we have a spiritual duty to see, touch, taste, and listen not only through the physical senses but through the finer ones of soul, to part the underbrush of own preconceived illusions and limitations to find the treasure around us and inside of us. Our senses are the gateway to deep experience, and even when one is impaired, the others are designed to become more acute to make up for it. The epitome of this phenomenon is author and activist Helen Keller; she could not see or hear, but she took in life to the fullest extent, fuller than most of us who have all of our senses intact. Upon visiting legendary dancer-choreographer Martha Graham's studio, she experienced the students' performance by feeling their vibrations on the floor; the photograph of Keller from that day exhibits a woman on fire with joy.

I once led a women's workshop with a focus on bliss and asked each person her definition of the word and an example of a time she might have experienced it in her own life. The majority of participants had a difficult time pulling an incident from memory, and a few confessed to never having felt ecstasy, much less understanding the mere definition of the word. *Bliss, ecstasy, felicity*—no matter which word we choose, indicates intense joy. The word ecstasy is from the Greek *ekstasis, "to stand outside oneself."* We have heard ourselves and others say, "I was beside myself," when describing something upsetting, yet many of us find it difficult to say the same about something positive.

The senses, like memory, can be rekindled and our worn-out nervous systems renewed; the capability to experience joy is inherent in each human being and can be awakened by simple nudges and willingness to feel—or feel again—without the distraction of noise, internal and external. Like Helen Keller, we too can feel the rhythm of life beneath our feet and find bliss for its own sake even in the presence of severe difficulty.

Last summer I spied a black butterfly on a cluster of rain-dappled blooms and was struck by the unique wing shape. When I inspected her closer, I realized that the butterfly had met with some trauma–her wings were torn, ripped out piece by piece, only half of her painted beauty still functioning. And function she did. From flower to flower, the butterfly paused to drink, up to speed as her other winged sisters. Aside from her ragged appearance, there was no indication of wounds or impaired flight. I found it hard to believe that such a delicate creature could survive so much loss, so much compromise, her very body maimed and half of what it once was. The butterfly not only continued to survive, but survived fully and exquisitely.

As humans, we too are torn, ripped, and storm-ravaged; sometimes we are bitten to shreds before narrow escape. We, too, find a way to go on, but not always with such grace and resolution. I doubt that the butterfly was lamenting her sad state as she supped in the garden, and what a beautiful thought for us to consider...crippled by life, fly! Drink deep! anyway...

# 4
# The Quest for Cool

## Whims of Changing Culture

Our bodies seem to fascinate us when we are very young. Most of us can probably remember a time when we were proud of our ponytails and potbellies, proud of the whole package. Until someone along the way led us to believe that the whole package was not what it "should be." *Stand up straight. Suck it in. Walk like a lady. Be still. Be quiet. Be everyone else's ideal of you.* The brief comment, silent disapproval, or schoolyard snicker becomes cellular memory long after the conscious mind forgets. The result is the inability to live consciously and most often, self-consciously.

There are countless cultures with their own unique shade, shape, and color of expression, yet what is "acceptable" is subject to region, day, month, year, decade, and century. Human beings can be fascinated by whim, and we forget that the human body and psyche cannot accommodate every whim that comes along. Just because someone thought that binding a woman's feet from infancy to adulthood to deform and cripple her was an ideal of beauty does not mean it was rational. Just because someone during the Inquisition decided that red-haired individuals were chosen by the Devil and subsequently tortured and/or killed did not mean it was sane. Just because religious text suggests that the left hand is sinful and someone decided that being left-handed indicates demonic tendencies and the person should be forced to learn to be right-handed did not mean it was sensible.

Having fiery tresses was once a spiritual crime; today, women are dying their hair instead of dying. A few decades ago, a skinny person was considered sick, boring, even ugly. It is a sad truth, but many of us are starving, cinching, cutting, pining, and self-loathing ourselves to death in the name of the latest whim that will soon be replaced by another.

## The Wilderness Within

If the body is indeed the temple of the soul, many of us have spirits that exist amid ruins. Culture's changing definitions of self-worth challenge our structures; year after year, decade after decade, winds of criticism and expectation assault our temples. Trends, mass marketing, celebrity worship, and the media invade our sanctuaries and hold us hostage to the idea that we are not good enough unless we are trimmed, painted, nipped and tucked, implanted, and ornamented. We learn the doctrine of comparison and deface our temples with dissatisfaction.

Self-negation leads to the loss of inner peace, sacred ground. The wild spirit inside of us becomes caged by societal obligation, and the pristine self is raped by the preferences of our culture. We conform to the "real world" and by doing so, lose the *real* world inside, the Self that is linked to our innate power and possibility. The independent Self needs no external reassurance of worth or feels a need to seek artificial, iconic inspiration. Nature alone can be our role model—she accepts her seasons and renews herself after devastating fires of loss; her resources of wisdom are ancient within her own autonomy. The wild self inevitably risks extinction in a society that values whim and fattens the ego while the spirit starves.

The body's sacredness has been forgotten in our high-tech world, but we all have the blueprints to our temples in our cellular memory. We know the floor plans intimately, innately; full restoration is possible. We must first be willing to relinquish layers of identity that we have acquired for social comfort, even social survival. We must consider the possibility that the preferences of mass consciousness are inessential and take responsibility for our own self-image. We can decide whether society's dysfunction should be our own. It is not easy being on the wrong side of the current cultural whim; most of us have disliked ourselves to some degree in the name of someone else's prejudice. Some of us have even betrayed our special qualities with pure self-hatred, but from this, we can gain freedom that is hard to come by. Once we survive our own persecution, the world and its mercurial opinions mean nothing.

In order to truly *be free* in our own skins, first we must own ourselves. No matter how frightening it may seem, we must be willing to untangle our true spirits from the nets of preconceived ideas, ideals, and expectations society places upon us from birth.

## The Age of Celebrity

Celebrities and others in the spotlight have always sent ripples throughout culture, and the rest of us have looked on in admiration, contempt, or reverence, sometimes imitating the good, bad, and the ugly. But in our current times, celebrity has jumped the boundaries of the arts and couture and has set up camp in our own neighborhoods. The advent of the reality show has given the average person a chance for fifteen minutes of fame; whether we are the proud parents of nineteen children, have a secret obsession, have a penchant for hiking naked through mosquito-dense jungles, or own a pawn shop in Las Vegas, it is our time to be famous or infamous, sometimes the latter being the most preferred. We reveal our most private moments on social media sites, our secret agonies on talk shows, and post videos on the World Wide Web with hopes that our home movie of the dog chasing its tail goes viral.

Excellence was once reserved for the few who had genuine drive and talent to be recognized for it; students who didn't make the grade were clearly shown their options which included being left behind a year or not being admitted to college despite ability to pay; young musicians with minimal ability were encouraged to do their best but not coaxed into the illusion that they possessed talent that could take them far; awards and certificates were handed out to the extraordinary not the majority for the sake of political correctness. Our young people have more opportunity for education and excellence than ever before, yet the truly exceptional children are falling through the cracks because singling out those gifted students seems unfair to the rest.

When a culture's standards decrease for the sake of the majority, the arts shrivel to hollow entertainment, the workforce becomes flooded with thousands of graduates with similar degrees, and excellence is exchanged for mediocrity or worse, sub-mediocrity.

## Dreams vs. Callings

In our desperation to be Somebody, we push our kids

into sports or entertainment, even if they do not show promise or interest. We tell them, "You can be anything," without backing it up with the difference between desire and aptitude. We all have dreams, but the difference between dreams and genuine callings is something that is not often clarified. A person with a tin ear may want to be the next Celine Dion, but wanting something does not give someone talent; having a desire to jump off a building and fly doesn't give us wings. Leading ourselves down a garden path of wanna-be accomplishment only hinders our true talents that lie elsewhere, and in turn, bankrupts culture.

Even with significant talent, fantasizing and talking about it does not nourish it and bring it forth. A calling differs from a dream because it is something that cannot be denied, something blazing from the core that propels us into action, keeps us up at night with gnawing inspiration and ambition, a living, breathing entity sitting on our shoulder pointing us in the right direction. Dreams are often driven by desire for notoriety while true callings are fueled by a do-or-die compulsion to bring forth the fire within. Artists of all disciplines, inventors, and visionaries coming from this place of pristine purpose are the treasures of our culture who refuse to sell their soul to anything of lesser value than their talent, jewels often tossed aside to make room for those with merely a dream who are willing to do anything for fame.

On the other side of the coin, true talent is often not encouraged; there is a prevailing attitude that refuses to acknowledge the path of creative accomplishment by summing it up as "the starving artist's road." Well, it's good someone didn't tell God it's not practical to create.

Imagine a world without books, music, film, design, philosophy, and abstract thinking that has birthed industry, invention, and technology...then imagine a world without a record of our history from the cave man to the modern world; thanks to the gifted artist, the storyteller, and the writer, history has been preserved. Someone wrote the song we share with a lover, the lullaby we sing to our babies, and the symphony that helps us make sense of our own place in this muddled world. Imagine a world without music. Or that film that changed our thinking. Or school books that educated us. Imagine a world without architecture and design, clothing and fashion. Someone designed our houses, the clothes on our backs, the plates we eat from. If not for the pioneers in photography, we would have no record of our kids or our marriages or our childhoods; if not for painters, generations before the photographic age would have had no record of their time on this earth, either. The inspired creative path, in all reality, is not only practical but vital.

Imagine a world without creators—individuals who believe that the very act of creating is a knee-jerk necessity not only for them, but for the world, even if it's just a trifling corner of it. Support the arts—take notice of something beautiful or truthful or evocative today; give thanks to those who continue to heed the calling so the rest of us can benefit. Let's not settle for mindlessness and junk-food culture. Let's keep the flame alive.

## Competitive Childhood vs. Creative Childhood

Thirty-five to a hundred years ago, childhood was a creative adventure, one that wasn't cluttered with minute-to-minute afterschool scheduling; kids played together without parents putting it on the calendar as play dates; kids informally played team sports and weren't tied to practice days, weekend games, or exorbitant uniform expenses; music, art, and dance lessons were a common part of life; sports idols were everyday people with everyday salaries. In short, yesterday's childhood was fueled on imagination, creative expression, and unregimented fun. Today's childhood is a calendar based on competitive activities; playing sports is more like a career than a hobby and the preferred "cool" thing to get your kid into. Playing team sports has its advantages, but when playing sports becomes a specific pigeon-holing mentality, that beautiful creativity that all kids are born with atrophies in the face of constant competitiveness and lack of imagination.

Today, half of the average Sunday newspaper is dedicated to professional sports. During the Olympics, we are bombarded with media hype and endless accounts about athletes, yet we rarely, if ever, hear about the excellence of our young musicians, dancers, or painters. There are no world-class violinists, scientists, or sculptors being endorsed for everything from cereal to chewing gum. Let's face it. Today's heroes fling a ball around, break records, and push their bodies to the limits. It may seem inspiring, feed the ego, and generate a lot of money, but hyping athletes just short of gods does nothing to further humankind. We are in a one-sided, sports-mentality culture that leaves very few options for our children to strive for greatness with their minds or creative talents.

Perhaps, if creative expression and visionary thinking were more supported and respected by the mass majority, we would encourage our kids to take up an instrument, pick up a paint brush, or look through a microscope. What could be *more powerful* than the act of creating something from nothing? Let's think about that next time we want our kids to dedicate much of their free time to a sport and nothing else. Playing a good game is fun, but it does nothing for humanity. Imagination, invention, preserving beauty, and discovery do. Let's bring some balance to our culture that has become obsessed with The Game and support perhaps a deeper excellence, one that future generations will benefit from.

# Part II

## Coming Back to Ourselves

# 5
# Antidote

## Redefining Success

Success, like beauty, is in the eye of the beholder. Individuals living comfortable middle-to-upper middle class lives may insist on referring to themselves as "poor" and an Olympic silver or bronze medalist might feel like a loser when the gold goes to someone else. A young mother in a Third World country may feel incredibly fortunate if she can feed her children or a writer with a day job who receives her first royalty check for a hundred dollars might feel more accomplished than if she had received a promotion at work.

The comparison trap snares us while most of us are still in grade school and usually begins with something small—an article of clothing we might not have in our wardrobe, the latest Gotta Get It Because It's Cool thing, or even a trendy hairstyle. When we're in school, we feel left out when we can't have what the next person has; as adults, we sometimes spend too much, put on airs, and never feel quite satisfied. Either way, there is a deep gnawing in the core of our lives that makes us restless. By our culture's standards, success hinges on luxury and status, and without either, the average person can spend an entire lifetime feeling like a failure, blind to true accomplishment beyond the distracting dissatisfaction of settling for less. Then there's also the other side of the coin: deep vacancy despite having success in the conventional sense.

If we pay close attention, our perception of achievement can shift through the years; perhaps our definition of personal success will be different on our deathbeds than it is now at this moment in time. Life's passages—illness, aging, loss, and births—have a sneaky and profound way of unraveling our tightest and most intricate patterns of perspective. It is common to experience a life-changing event that knocks the wind out of us and makes us take a good look at what is truly important. We vow to make changes in our lives, be more mindful, and respond to life in a different way. One week, one month, or one year may go by before the effects wear off, and without even noticing, we slip back into the same fast lane—sometimes faster than before—and forget the clarity we gained during crisis or transition.

In a holistic sense, true success involves the body, mind, and spirit, and each domain has its own set of requirements. After a while, we may ask ourselves if we want to appear happy or truly *be* happy. Sometimes playing the game no longer brings fulfillment, only physical and mental exhaustion. That is when we wake up and realize we deserve the real thing.

Redefining success is not a snap decision, something we just decide to do. Rather, it is a slow awakening from a very fitful sleep. It takes true, deep, gut-wrenching, unflinching fortitude to face the illusions of society and question their validity. Instead of questioning where we have fallen short or why we are not good enough, for once, let's question the source of our discontent, see the comparison trap for what it really is, and find a way out of it.

My husband's Uncle Lou was a brilliant man who lived by his own accord in a small room filled with books and few possessions. He attended Yale University, corresponded with Einstein, and saw life through abstract eyes. He authored books and then destroyed his creations when they were finished simply because he felt he had reached his goal. He tuned out the family gossip and judgment and found contentment in his own stark autonomy.

This man's example is inspiring not because he chose to be a minimalist or an author just for his own eyes but for the simple fact that he did not place cultural expectation above *his own requirements* for contentment.

If cultural guidelines and illusions did not factor in our decisions, how would our requirements for happiness change? What would shift in our lives if there was nothing and no one molding our path?

**Honesty with Self**

Honesty with ourselves can be the most painful kind of truth; it can also bring the deepest freedom. Self-honesty is the key in finding our own heartbeat amidst the roar of Shoulds and Don'ts passed down to us from well-meaning loved ones and mentors. Honesty with ourselves demands that we have the courage to face and question generational legacy. Questioning the path hewn for us can put the burden of guilt upon us, as if the very act denotes disrespect for our blood and cultural ties. In reality, it simply opens the door to our own expansion.

Self-honesty includes forthrightness about our emotions, dissatisfaction, the past, disappointments, longings, lost selves, abandoned talents, excuses, relationships, addictive patterns, and everything else that we tend to keep at bay. It can shake up our very foundations, crumble what we believed to be true, and after everything's said and done, enable us to see the Self we compromised in the name of all that does not allow room for our highest good. The effort can seem monumental if we approach it intellectually, but when we simply make a commitment to *allow* the feelings to be felt and the realizations to surface, the compromised Self can test the waters and begin to emerge. Allowance can be the greatest tool in our evolutionary journey, a deep acceptance *of* and value *for* ourselves at the core level. It is nothing less than a state of grace, an autumnal letting-go much like the trees relinquishing outgrown leaves; the bare honesty of our truths can be a beautiful thing. Self-honesty distills our lives down to bare essence. Concentration of priority and integrity is worth the discomfort of detaching ourselves from what we thought was best for us.

What seemed ideal for us ten or twenty years ago may not apply as we get older. Contentment and true success is not a one-size-fits-all plan but a deeply personal, individual, and *sacred* journey. A wise person once advised me, "Don't be afraid to make your own rules and then don't be afraid to break them." Often, breaking our own rules can be the very key that frees us from both inherited and acquired illusion.

What would happen if we were honest with ourselves at this moment? What emotions prowling the perimeter would show themselves? What needs would demand tending to? Could we finally call a truce with our mistakes and make peace with ourselves? Could we face the demons in our hearts and realize they can teach us something invaluable?

What could we finally let go of in order to gain something far more valuable?

## Finding True Priorities

Those old, clichéd questions like "If the house was burning down, what would you save?" or "If you had a year to live, how would you live it?" can be good priority sorters. During the hurricane season last year, most residents of the East Coast of the United States did not have to ask themselves these questions to get clarity about what really mattered to them. Many of us were without power for days, weeks, some over a month, and most of us had an opportunity to take inventory of what we deemed valuable in our lives. Over the course of a few days, I got to know my life and my husband's face by candlelight as we listened to 1930s radio shows on our hand-crank, swapped stories, and nestled in our dark house like two swallows in the eaves. We remembered the luxury of running water, shampoo, washing dishes, and the night light in our bedroom; we offered humble gratitude for living in a part of the world where we take these things for granted every hour of the day.

Months later, pockets of our home state are still struggling to bounce back after towns, homes, businesses, and lives were wiped out. Our lights went back on within a week; our routine resumed little by little, but we were able to perceive clearer than ever before the importance of seeing life, circumstances, people, divisions, even our own souls, in a softer light and felt the inclination to create more meaningful lives.

Hopefully, many of us do not need the loss of a home or the the death of a loved one to help us reposition our priorities; with a bit of luck, we won't experience a life-threatening or life-altering illness before we can make time for our bodies and psyches, and most of all, stillness. Putting ourselves back in the equation is not selfish or impossible. It is necessary.

What would happen if every one of us on this planet healed from our life-wounds, took care of the trinity (body, mind, and soul), got out of our own way, stopped making excuses, lived through heart rather than ego, and mended the broken pieces of the compromised Self? Healing our own individual lives helps to contribute to the healing of the whole, a drop of clean water in a stagnant pond.

What would happen if we took responsibility for own wellbeing? What would happen if we reserved a corner of our lives exclusively for us? Contrary to many of our fears and self-judgments, we would not stop caring for those we love, providing for our families, raising our kids with integrity and generosity, or succeeding at our work; we would have more soul-energy, more hope, more incentive, and more gifts to pass on.

Running ourselves ragged, never saying "no," and being everything to everyone leads to physical exhaustion, emotional unavailability, mental burnout, and soul-numbness. In all logic, how could this have a positive ripple-effect on our children? Our partnerships, loved ones, and careers? Anxiety, irritability, chronic illness, circumstantial depression, and loss of self often go hand-in-hand with priorities that have little to do with us and everything about everyone else. In the long run, honoring our place in our own lives can only benefit everyone around us. Self-care has long been confused with selfishness, but there is a big difference between the two. Self-care allows us to put ourselves *on* the priority list; selfishness prompts us to forget about everyone else on that list. Self-care inspires others; selfishness drains.

Rearranging priorities might take a while to figure out. It may also be very difficult. We might wrestle with guilt. Some people in our lives might think we've gone crazy. Transforming is the hardest job we will ever do, but it is doable. It is worth it. If we make it so.

For the heck of it, take a pen and a piece of paper (or go on the computer) and write down your top priorities for any given day. Then list your top priorities in life, in detail. Go over both lists separately and then number them according to importance. After scanning your lists, put a check by anything regardless of importance or practicality that is standing between you and a more meaningful life, you and more time, you and more moments of contentment, you and what you hunger for. Take a week or a month to sit with your lists and see if anything is added or deleted over that time; after a while, once again, number each priority in importance and see if your lists differ. Be honest with yourself. There is no right and wrong, only your truth.

## Inner Transitions

Questioning, finding true priorities, and learning to be with our whole selves without distraction may take months or years; it may even feel terrifying. Transitions aren't easy for any of us, animals and plants included. Animals prepare for winter in haste; gardens wind down, leaves and petals curling in ochre, fuchsia cheeks of the roses tinged with rust.

Nationally, we are on the threshold of many changes and globally, we stand on a fiery edge with rage burning through the Middle East as I type. It's a scary time on planet Earth, and we each must do what we need to do in order to remain centered, defiant flames against strengthening winds.

"If transitions are like high bridges," a wise friend once said, "then just don't look down." Her clever advice was timely and spot-on. A lot of energy is squandered by anticipating the other side, rushing the journey, worrying ourselves sick about the empty space (the unknown?) swirling beneath us...when in reality, all we can do is take one step at a time until we reach the other end, hopefully intact and better for the crossing.

Young adulthood, going to university, entering or leaving a partnership, beginning or ending a career, starting a family, midlife, retirement, burying parents—we experience many transitions as we go through life, and changing consciousness can be among the most challenging and fear-producing. We can only feel our way through it daily. Some days we intentionally look down from the bridge and admire the view from this time in our lives, while on others we panic when we realize we are halfway across and

and there is no going back, no doing over again, only forward, even when the way is dark and storm-blind.

None of us know what waits on the other side of the bridge—and perhaps, we can find comfort in knowing that it is a mystery, one we might be content with not solving. We got this far, didn't we? There is a lot to feel proud, humbled, and good about as we look out into the darkness and put forth willingness to trust the rest of the journey.

Patience with ourselves can help us transition, and nature is our best mentor. Nature is the master of timing. Trees and all growing things wait, know how to rest after bursting forth and producing something that will never be seen again in quite the same way. Gardeners and farmers play the waiting game with grace, charts of when-to-plant-what engraved on their hearts and fingernails stained from the effort. Animals go with the flow, living mainly on intuition and observation, thinking nothing beyond the moment at hand. Unborn babies are angels of divine timing, waiting in the dark under the Great Mother's heartbeat. Creating a new consciousness and a new approach to life is a holy act, one we cannot rush. Waiting is the awkward, grungy step-sister of creating, the muse's mundane shadow self who brings out the worst and best in any person who learns her sometimes-tortuous ways.

The grape and the wine maker know that timing is everything, and on days when we stomp our feet with frustration and impatience, we can remember the wisdom of the vine: drink deeply the rain, relish the sun's gold, age beautifully and succulently, trust the Tender's hands and the dark cellar where dust and years accumulate to see us to greatness.

## Re-awakening the Senses

Sensation and the finer qualities of heart and spirit make life worth living. Children respond to life without reservation, senses new and razor-sharp. Our often-flatlined adult senses make us go through life skimming the surface, looking but not seeing, hearing but not quite listening, consuming but not really tasting. Most of us need a fresh perspective, and it's never too late to truly feel again. Waking up body and spirit does not require lengthy vacations, mountain retreats, or a perfect life.

Small things approached with mindfulness can turn an ordinary day into one that glints with the occasional flash of beauty and meaning, even delight. The quickest way to be totally in the moment (not anticipating the future, not dwelling on the past) is through the blessing of our five senses.

## See

That old saying, *the eyes are the windows to the soul* can imply much more than discernment of character. Those of us who are blessed with the sense of sight can take it for granted and never really fine-tune our eyes to see nuances of beauty, detail, or color. Caught up in a busy day, we might fail to see something spectacular, even if we are looking right at it. Visual artists often capture what goes unnoticed, bringing our scattered attention to a stillpoint through art or photograph, gently tapping us on the shoulder with the reminder, "Look at *this*...look at what you're missing."

The eyes *are* windows to the soul—our souls. They are portals that can usher us into a different perspective, shock us awake with hidden beauty, and make us smile with subtle but profound epiphany. There are worlds within our mundane world, realms accessible with the naked eye if we remember to *see* when we look. We can do it while we're stopped in traffic or at a light, on our lunch breaks, during a dental visit, while watching the television, and just about anywhere. A seemingly monotonous day can turn magical with just a little more seeing in our looking. As painters know, everything in the 3-D world has layers of depth, color, hue, shape, light, shadow, and texture, and these are only the physical attributes. Look even deeper and we can find the heart of just about anything.

The power of observation is something that can bring us upliftment or agitation, depending upon intention. It is human inclination to notice other people and sometimes judge them by how they're dressed, what they look like, how they speak, and how they interact with us. We might be too busy to notice a tree blazing in October scarlet but pick up on details of the person who cut in front of us on line at the minimart. It's a good chance that we notice his balding spot, the Band-Aid on his left elbow, and his untied tennis shoe. What would happen if we decided to put this eye for detail for better use and really take in the magnificence surrounding us daily?

Even the most chaotic and uninteresting places have snippets of beauty: an urban courtyard littered with garbage most likely will have brave, determined sprigs of green or flowers blooming through a crack in the cement. The window in a dentist's office might offer a corner of shocking blue sky, a bird feeder, a metallic skyline reflecting clouds, or patterns of rain. Stopped at a light we might notice a beautiful face in the crowd, a smiling little girl, or a pigeon with beautiful shimmers of color. There is beauty to be acknowledged everywhere if we have eyes to recognize it.

The lovely, rare, hidden, and intriguing are gifts and like many gifts, often taken for granted or brushed off in the name of Busy. "I'll notice it tomorrow," we might think to ourselves. But why not notice what today has to offer? William Blake's "Catch joy as it flies..." is sage advice.

**Affirmation**: *At my journey's end, ignoring beauty will not be one of my regrets.*

### *Hear*

Hearing a bird's voice at dawn, Chopin's *Nocturnes*, or a lover's whisper is a privilege most of us don't think about that often. The power of hearing can bring us pleasure or alert us to danger; the power of listening can fill up the empty spaces in our lives and create deep bonds between souls. Even those who are hearing-challenged can listen and hear what the rest of us miss with near-perfect auditory faculties.

Hearing, like other senses, is multidimensional and

penetrates layers of perception. There is a lot to be heard in the silence between sentences, between the notes of a song, and the space between heartbeats. Perhaps, listening to ourselves is the most valuable capability we can hone, and using our physical ears is a good place to start.

Being tuned into our surroundings is not as easy as we might believe. In our age of noise, it is common to have the television or radio blasting and not be aware of it; sometimes we even sleep through it. How often do we find ourselves tapping our feet to a catchy song but fail to listen to the lyrics, or hear the dawn ignite with birdsong but fail to pick out individual birds in the chorus? As humans equipped with the blessings of sensual response, we have found infinite ways to deprive ourselves of deep listening.

What are a few of your favorite sounds? Ocean waves? Your child's laughter? Wind in the trees? Hustle and bustle of a city? We can truly listen anywhere...at work, lying in bed, at a child's Little League game, walking in the park, sitting with our own thoughts. Once we tune in to what we love, notice what we don't care for, and invite the world into our listening, the inner sounds will become clearer. What thoughts can you hear inside the private sanctuary of your own mind? What do you hear in your memories? Your dreams at night?

The goal is to fully take in our immediate, external world and then be able to go to the next layer and listen to the sounds of our own inner space; ultimately, to be able to listen even further and find the deepest resonance possible, the song of the soul... and then sing it back to the world.

**Affirmation**: *I listen to all that life has to offer.*

## *Feel*

Touch is the sense that is a double-edged sword; we can feel exquisite pleasure or excruciating pain. Our skin is the doorway to millions of nerve endings forming a metropolis of sensation. Touch can harm or heal, abuse or bless. Touch connects us to each other and can be the most powerful form of communication we have. Parent and child, lover and beloved, human and animal, the bonds we create through touch are sacred ones.

As our energy fans out in multiple directions, touch, along with the other senses, gets lost in the shuffle. We take showers but may not actually feel the water on our skin or notice a lover's passing caress yet min-

or aches and pains might prompt us to take a pain-killer. In our modern age, our feel-good sensation is compromised while we jump to numb pain's subtle messages.

Many of us can remember being children delighting in the simple joy of feeling sand through our fingers—warm giving way to cool as we reach down deeper into beach sand or sand box. Soda bubbles fizzing on our tongues. Wind against our faces from an open car window. Our sense of touch pulsed with clarity, and everything felt new against our tender skins. As adults, the intensity of feeling is usually at an apex when we fall madly in love, give birth, or grieve. During most of life between these passages, our sense of touch can be less than memorable.

One of the easiest ways to get in touch with our sense of touch is to seek fabrics that feel good against the skin: satin, silk, soft cotton, suede, broken-in denim. Luxurious sheets, a winter blanket or robe, well-worn jeans, plush slippers. Another is taking a few extra minutes to enjoy the usually-hurried morning or evening shower; feel the spray against your face. Run cool water over your hands on a hot day; really take notice of the silken stream between your fingers, on your palms, against your wrists. Memorize a loved one's touch, their texture of skin on the palm of the hand, cheek, and forearm. Pet your animal companion, enjoying the soft-belly rub as much as they do. Feeling alive begins by *feeling*.

**Affirmation**: *I touch life and allow life to touch me.*

### *Smell*

Our perception of smell is rooted in the limbic portion of the human brain, the oldest part of the brain which governs deep memory, emotional response, and many other functions. It is responsible for prompting associations through aroma, fragrance, or odor from an individual's memory bank…Mom's muffins fresh from the oven, summer mint clipped from a patio garden, the acridness of bleach, cherry lip balm, cigarette smoke, ocean air. The cells of our being connect memory and emotion most profoundly through the sense of smell.

Anyone who has temporarily lost this sense from a miserable cold or sinus infection knows how flat life becomes without the ability to enjoy the food on the plate or sense the natural world such as ozone after a good rain. Simply and purely, the sense of smell gives us delight, and despite its immediacy, can also be a casualty as we wrestle with the daily The To-Do List. Most of us can say which scents remind us of childhood, first love, and people we care about, but what would you say if someone asked you to name the smells you associate with yourself and your daily routine? What do you take notice of in your living space, work place, or neighborhood café? Which ones bring you passing pleasure or discontent?

To the attentive nose, the world can be a wondrous place. Bakeries, spice markets, freshly-mowed summer fields, baby shampoo, hot cocoa, fresh sheets, a mountain snowfall, simmering soup, morning coffee. Aromas and perfumes of our days can be powerful matchmakers in our quest to fall in love again with our lives. Why don't we take a few seconds between tasks and simply inhale? And then again, this time deeply. Let's notice the wiles of our favorite soap or hand lotion, a loved one's shower-fresh hair; let's toss out harsh chemical cleaners and use something more environmentally-friendly that will leave our kitchens smelling of lavender or lemongrass; let's smell that piece of chocolate we pop under the tongue and set off some happy chemicals in our brains. Let's start living more like our dogs and go through life with busy noses. We'll be better for it.

**Affirmation**: *I breathe in the beautiful fragrance of my life.*

### *Taste*

Very few would disagree that taste is high on the list of life's blissful gifts. Sweet, salty, bitter, and sour swirl harmonious magic on our tongues, inviting nourishment of body and soul. In the 21$^{st}$ Century, those of us who are fortunate enough to answer our hunger three times a day keep our bellies full, but can we say the same for our spirits? Many of us eat when we're hungry, physically or emotionally, yet how many of us can say we truly feel satiated? How often do we mollify a craving yet feel a deep hunger in the core of our solar plexus that has nothing to do with bodily sustenance? For a moment, a heavenly response from our taste buds invites us to forget work, unpaid bills, and broken hearts; when we're happy, it bids us to celebrate our joy in every morsel.

Like all senses, taste branches into unseen dimensions. Taste acts as a bridge between food and raw emotion. Some of us, especially women, can experience deep emotional pain, perhaps even sudden tears, when we reach for food in an attempt to fill an inner void. Sometimes one bite of sweetness will open the dam and we will feel everything we have numbed ourselves to. For a brief moment, our sense of taste gives us permission to feel what is otherwise too painful.

Food addiction and obesity are very common challenges during our modern age, and unlike other compulsive issues, intricately entwined with core survival; we can live without alcohol, illegal drugs, gambling, spending, and sex, but we cannot live without food. The quest for satiety and immediate fulfillment fails to nourish us nutritionally as well as spiritually.

If we can make a commitment to rediscovering taste's biological and divine purpose—that of catalyzing nourishment—perhaps we can heal our starving spirits while meeting the body's complex biochemical needs. Too many of us rush our meals, eat on the run, eat with the television on or while talking on the phone, or overeat instead of resolving frustrations, and in doing so, literally and metaphorically become oblivious to all the flavors life has to offer us.

What if we stopped seeing food as reward and emotional security and saw it as a gateway to vitality? What if we slowed down and let our taste buds lead us to true nourishment of body, mind, and spirit? What if preparing and consuming food became a form of prayer instead of an obligation? What if we took a bite out of life without fear and over-analysis? What if we saw a myriad of choices in the banquet rather than restrictions and deprivation?

**Affirmation**: *I eat to nourish my body, and I taste to nourish my soul.*

## Re-introduction to Self

Self and self are two sides of the same coin, the difference between the two being a simple matter of *conscious*ness. The lower-case self is our everyday self—the self that survives on autopilot, conforms to expectations, and gets snagged on generational illusion. The true Self is the one that is compromised by the everyday self, the being that keeps our abandoned callings and talents for safekeeping, the unaffected and wild individual whose autonomy is never sacrificed for the sake of acceptance by the pack. This Self lives in the heart of our deepest vulnerability. It is capable of responding to life with sensual intensity while maintaining prudence, diving into each day with eagerness and gratitude while knowing stillness. It is what some call the higher self or in ancient times, the *genius* or guiding spirit that nudges us closer to reaching our earthly potential. The Self is most clearly seen in babies and children before they begin to fully experience the social dynamic of interaction with friends, school peers, and siblings. In other words, before the comparison trap snaps shut and well-intended generational anticipation sets in.

The Self is the part of us that finds it instinctive to create and assures that this *innate* energy is honored and allowed to express itself. The Self creates without thought or self-consciousness, making something from nothing much like a spider spinning everything she needs from her own body. The process of creation is independent of external influence and is not affected by the prospect of end results or product. The bird sings at dawn for its own delight just as the true artist molds clay or words for his/her own inborn hunger to express what everyday language cannot.

Many Selves are lost in the survival of the self; too many die with no hope of resurrection. Creative impulse, like muscle tissue, can atrophy if not used, and worse, can be extinguished if it gets snarled in worldly concerns of grotesque ambition. On the practical level, creativity inspires us to prepare beautiful food, provide an inviting and safe haven for ourselves and our loved ones, even express individuality through choices of clothing and personal style. We do not need to paint, sing, or dance in order to live creatively— the Self sees everyday tasks as opportunities to express its uniqueness.

The Self is also the lover within, the part of us that loves without walls; it rarely knows fear, and when it does, loves anyway. The Self allows pleasure and personal integrity to dwell within the body without compromise. The busier our lives become and the more directions in which we are pulled, the lover within can wither like a plant without light. In our modern world, views on sexuality are broadening to such an extent that the lines that used to divide and define our sexual behavior are almost erased. In this age of sexual freedom that declares "anything goes and everything's okay," inhibition has been unchained but unfortunately has created an emotional chasm between lover and beloved. In order to rediscover Eden, we have to cut through all the distracting layers and again find the true essence of the beloved. Beneath sexual experimentation, novelties, and hollow trends, there is a naked soul and a beating heart of the lover, and it can only be found when we remember that making love is a gift. It is a gift to have a body that can be an instrument of love. It is a gift to bless another human being with ecstasy. It is a gift to know another person as only a lover can. When we stand naked in front of another human being, we are giving all that we came into this life with and the only thing we truly own until death—the body, the temple of the soul. We would never enter a place of worship with selfish motivation or momentary lust for gratification. We would not dirty the purity of a place of holiness with disrespect or dishonor, or enter with a false heart. Yet we do these things to our lovers and allow our lovers to do the same to us. In our age of disease, promiscuity and isolation, we must once again see the body and the lover within as sacred instruments, holy places, and gifts not to be given in a moment's carelessness or hurriedness.

**Affirmation**: *I make room for my true Self in my life; I create and love with complete and uncompromised honesty.*

## Allowing for Imperfection

It is a human tendency to strive for perfection, and despite the odds and all logic, we invest time, energy, money, and sometimes our very wellbeing in the wild goose chase. Fortunately, we did not come into the world to be perfect, only human. Embracing our human qualities and flaws equally may take years of dedicated intention and could possibly be the missing link for a happier life.

Humans are paradoxical—intolerant to imperfection in ourselves and others yet prize it and reserve it for certain things in life. We value distressed furniture, hand-blown glass blemished with trapped air bubbles, the line of weathered and twisted oaks, old houses, haphazard hair trends, faded antiques, ripped denim to name a few.

Perfection is in the eye of the beholder but is usually suggested to us from outside sources. What if we set our own idea of perfection which includes imperfection? What if we focused on the dynamic of the two side by side and saw a dance of harmony? What if we realized that imperfection is an intricate part of the perfect whole? What if reaching perfection is simply allowing for imperfection? What if living a perfect life simply meant accepting what is not?

# 6

# Taking Inventory

## Making a Commitment

Once we realize it is our birthright to have more of *us* in our lives, to honor the Self, and put our abandoned priorities back on The To-Do List, we can make a simple commitment to following through. Making a commitment means we will protect our wellbeing the same way we protect our kids, loved ones, and prized possessions. It means we will never dishonor it again in the name of Busy or by saying "yes" when we need to say "no." It means that we respect *what* we love as much as *who* we love. It means that our feelings, bodies, psyches, callings, and time matter as much as everything else. It means we are committed to improving our own lives and not waiting for the perfect time and circumstances to do it. It means we realize that all we are truly guaranteed is Now, and now is the time.

Commitment to our own wellbeing is just as sacred as making a commitment to marriage, children, a spiritual path, or career. Our relationship with ourselves is critical because we live in our skins 24/7. We can't leave the relationship when things get tough. We can't take a vacation. We can't trade it in for another. It's the most important relationship in our lives and ultimately determines the quality of all our other relationships. Sometimes we lose touch with ourselves so much that we feel disconnected from our true feelings and need a nudge to see the whole picture.

In the next section you will find a questionnaire you will probably think you don't have time for, and the more you think you don't have time for it, the more you need to fill it out. Make that call later; water the plants another time; clean the kitchen tomorrow. Don't worry if you can only complete a few questions a day...take a month if you need to complete it. Right now, you are the priority. Grab a pen and some paper and be willing to sit with yourself and the questions. Most of all, be willing to respect yourself enough to be brutally honest. This is for your eyes only, and there are no right or wrong answers.

# Questionnaire

1. When was the last time you can truly say you have felt content in your life?

2. What do you need personally in order to feel content? List your answers. Be sure to include what you might think are "small" things.

3. What made you feel safe and happy as a child? If you didn't actually have these things or circumstances, what would have made you feel safe and happy?

4. What life event, if any, changed how you think about yourself, the world, or both? How did you think before the event and how did you think after it?

5. In the course of a day, how often are you aware of how you feel physically? How often do you address your physical issues?

6. Do you often feel irritable, angry, or frustrated? Do you stuff down these emotions or take them out on those nearest to you?

7. Do you feel like your life is not in your own hands? Do you feel that circumstances or other people control your decision-making?

8. How much on your To-Do list is about meeting the needs of others?

9. Do you feel guilty when you say "No?" Are you easily talked into "Yes?"

10. Do you dream of escaping your life?

Spiritual Famine in the Age of Plenty

11. If you had one day to focus just on yourself, would you take it? Could you do it without feeling selfish? How would you spend it?

12. When you are extremely upset, what is the first thing you do?

13. Do you reach for food when you are emotional?

14. What is your secret, never-told-anyone dream? It does not matter how impossible it may be.

15. Which dreams have not come true? Which ones have? Did the ones that came true leave you feeling disappointed?

16. What talents do you believe have been sacrificed for survival, family obligations, or lack of confidence?

17. If no one would notice if you failed, what would you try?

18. If your mind is active in the middle of the night, what thoughts keep you awake? Write down the usual culprits.

19. What in your day brings you joy?

20. Do you catch yourself longing for the days of your youth? If so, what age? What is it about that time you miss?

21. Do you have any regrets? Practical, occupational, emotional, or financial? List any or all. What would you do differently?

22. What do *you* want most from life?

23. Can you say that you have done right by yourself? Do you show your physical health, emotions, and spirit the same integrity you show others in your life?

24. Do you feel disappointed with yourself? If so, why? If you asked a friend the same question, how would you respond to the same answer?

25. Have you been deeply in love?

26. Do you truly feel loved? By family? By your partner? Friends?

27. Do you *feel* appreciated? How do others show this?

28. What about yourself would others be surprised to learn? Have you intentionally kept this from them? If so, why?

29. How much does fear play in your major life decisions?

30. How much does outside opinion play in your decisions?

31. If you had a month to live, what would you change about your life or circumstances?

32. When was the last time you felt blissful?

33. If you could change three things about the world, what would you change? Can you apply these three things to your own life

and make a difference in your corner of the world?

34. How much does nutrition play in your diet?

35. Do you feel a connection between the earth and your eating habits?

36. When was the last time you savored a meal?

37. Do you find yourself rushing even on your days off?

38. Do you feel guilty if you don't answer the phone every time it rings?

39. Do you feel that if you sit down you won't get up?

40. Do you listen to your body's pain signals?

41. Can you feel pleasure—eating, making love, being pampered? Or do you find yourself distracted or numb?

42. What are your favorite things in nature?

43. What catches your eye and what do you find beautiful? Is beauty necessary to your wellbeing? Do you make time for beauty?

44. What relationships in your life feel obligatory? There is no right or wrong answer.

45. What would happen if you were unable to get out of bed for a while? Do other people depend upon you so much that they would have a hard time being responsible for getting things done?

46. Do you need to be everything to everyone? If so, how much does this have to do with how you feel about yourself? Do you need to be needed?

47. If your answer did not include other people, what gives you a sense of purpose in life?

48. Do you find yourself settling for less emotionally?

49. What is your spirit crying out for at this time in your life?

50. What is your definition of recreation? Do you make time for it?

51. Do you make time to nourish your spiritual life? What feeds your soul?

52. Do you underestimate your importance? If so, what would enable you to see your contribution as valuable?

53. Do you need more passion, romance, or loving in your life?

54. Do you feel flatlined emotionally?

55. If you died today, what in your life would feel unfinished?

56. Can you do "nothing" and feel it's okay?

57. What would you ask for if you allowed yourself to?

58. What do you look forward to?

59. What makes you feel cared for? Would you consider doing this for yourself without feeling self-centered?

60. Do you believe the best of life is behind you or yet to come? Is it now? With a few changes, *could* it be now? If so, what would need to change?

# 7

# $\mathfrak{B}$aby Steps to Bliss

## Daily Delights

When we see the word *vacation* we usually conjure images of our favorite places, time to spare, carefree long days and even longer nights, good food, good company, and not having to be anywhere. The opportunity to relax is the idea. Many of us have vacation time but come back to our lives feeling exhausted while others rarely get time away and long for it. Vacation is a mindset, turning off obligation and putting down our concerns, and the good news is that we don't actually have to go on vacation to reap the benefits of the same intention.

Meditators claim that twenty minutes of calming the mind and body is equal to a two hour nap. Deep breathers believe that a few, mindful breaths daily may prolong life. Lovers swear that making love decreases their pain levels and lifts their moods. Meditation, breathwork, and an active sex life may actually contribute to our wellbeing yet many of us cannot find time or energy for it. This is where we stop aiming for ideal circumstances and take what I call mini vacations which can help to reset a frazzled nervous system and provide much-needed positivity. Here's a list of 5 minute, 20 minute, and 1 hour mental "vacations" you may want to try. Over the course of a day, you might be surprised how much impact these mini de-stressors have on overall wellbeing.

### For just 5 minutes...

-*Take a worry break*. No matter what problems plague you, vow to take five minutes to not focus on them. If you can manage it, go ten minutes. Each time a worry taps you on the shoulder, remind yourself that your five or ten minutes aren't up yet. Do this as often as you like and see how much time you can devote to not giving in to worry.

-*Daydream.* That's right, pick something absolutely delightful and fantasize about it. Daydreaming can release endorphins and help relax the body. As kids, we daydreamed all the time. As adults, it may seem odd, but it's a great five minute vacation.

-*Breathe in some beauty.* Clip a fragrant flower, put a dab of essential oil on a tissue, or spritz your favorite scent on your hand and breathe deeply, deliberately, sensually.

-*Stay in the here and now.* Most of us spend our lives with the past or future orbiting our minds. Take five minutes to be totally in the Now. Take notice of your surroundings, even at work...take in details of small things like pens, car keys, clothing patterns, pictures on the wall, a tree outside the window. Take notice of smells, sounds, textures, temperature, anything and everything that will keep your mind drifting to the future, the past, and what you have to accomplish today.

*-Do something you love.* Listen to a favorite song. Eat a bite of dark chocolate and taste it for as long as you can. Open that book you have no time for and just read a page or two. Doodle. Call someone you haven't called in a while because you don't have time and say, "I only have five minutes, but I wanted to say 'hello'." Most often we don't do what we love because we think we need an allotment of time for it, but five minutes here or there doing something that gives us joy is five more minutes of something good in our day.

## For just 20 minutes...

*-Forget a grievance.* Take twenty minutes (time it if you wish) to make the decision to be happy. Vow to take twenty minutes to set aside resentment, frustration, grief, anger, and agitation and replace it with a lighter attitude. Say to yourself, "This is my twenty minutes to be happy. I can be <u>mad</u> (insert your own word) later."

*-Take a footbath.* If you're sitting at the computer, on the phone, watching the tube, or sitting and doing work at home, fill a basin of warm or hot water, add a dash of Epsom salts or sea salt, and a splash of bubble bath or essential oil and soak your feet. We don't

realize how much tension we carry in our feet and how much we can relax from a good footbath. It's also great to do before going to sleep.

-*Choose a mantra.* A mantra is a phrase or word used in meditation; it can be voiced out loud or kept within the sanctity our own thoughts. Choose a word or phrase that makes you feel good and mentally repeat it. It might feel odd if you've never done this before, but give it a try. You can do it at work, in the car, on the subway, at the supermarket, wherever you go. After a few minutes, your chosen feel-good word or phrase will run in the background of your thought process and work its magic. Here are a few suggestions: *I am at peace. Peace. I am loved. I love myself. Safe and sound. Beauty. All is well. Hope. Here and Now. Joy.* If you are religious, add something of your faith to your mantra or repeat part of a prayer.

-*Be hopeful.* Even if your world is falling apart, believe the best is about to happen or your path is paved with miracles. Invite only good into your space and refuse to believe any differently for just twenty minutes. Your immune system will thank you.

**For just an hour...**

*-Unless you're on call for work or a dire situation, don't answer your phone...ALL phones apply.* Voicemail is there to take messages. Let it. Turn off all sounds that alert you to a call or text. Take sixty minutes to be unavailable. Be prepared to be shocked...the world will go on; and you will have an hour without the obligation of constant contact. No guilt allowed or it defeats the purpose.

*-Unplug completely.* For an hour, go offline, don't watch TV, don't listen to the radio, don't text or talk on the phone and just be in your corner of the world without being pulled into the rest of it.

*-Be your own best friend.* This means that for one hour, you will try your best to treat yourself with care...smile every time you see your reflection; if you think a self-negating thought, replace it with a positive one; do something you ordinarily don't make time for; enjoy your own company; think about your accomplishments and everything you feel good about in your life; give yourself a hand or foot massage. The possibilities are endless and usually springboard from things you would readily do for a good friend but not necessarily yourself.

*-Break your own rules.* For one hour, branch out of

your comfort zone in some way. If you're not social, say "hello" to a total stranger; if you are usually a hands-on worrywart in relation to loved ones, pull back and let go; if you don't like to cook, make something to eat; if you pride yourself on how you can go-go-go but feel tired, take a catnap. You get the idea.

## Doing the "Unthinkable"

Once you are able to apply a few of the above-mentioned suggestions into your daily life, you might want to graduate to the next level of coming back to yourself. In today's world, most of us can't go an hour much less a day or a week without being tied to the usual trappings of technology, distraction, and running ourselves ragged. No matter how we dream of an unplugged life, in all reality, it just isn't practical or desired in the long run. This is where doing the "unthinkable" can let us have our cake and eat it, too. I invite you to give yourself some new experiences and mindsets with the following good-for-your-wellbeing ideas:

### For just one day...

-*Take an email sabbatical.* For one day, don't check

or answer any email.

*-Ditch your cell phone.* For one day, don't use your cell phone. Tell your important contacts that you will not be available for the day.

*-Don't turn on the television or radio.* Unplug from the media, forget the news, don't listen to anything but your own thoughts and try to make them good.

*-Live in the 19$^{th}$ Century.* Turn off the usual light sources and enjoy a gentler glow. Light some candles, turn on some LED candles (safer), or use an oil lamp over supper. Take it into the rest of your evening and avoid the television, computer, radio, phone/cell phone, Internet, etc. If you live with other people, have a few laughs, good conversation, play a game, catch up on rest, sit and be with the night.

*-Eat better.* Just for a day, eat more salads, home-cooked food, and eat fruit if your sweet tooth needs a kick. Back to basics.

*-Practice saying "No."* If you truly want to say "No" but feel you must say "Yes," try "No" on for size.

-*Don't rush inside.* Even if you are running late and going through frazzled motions, make an attempt to not rush inside. Running inside even when we know we're stopped in traffic won't get us to our destinations any quicker but will raise our stress hormones. Practice inner stillness even when in motion.

## Try it for a week...

-*Go offline*. Extend that email sabbatical to an Internet sabbatical. Notify your contacts, set your email to vacation response and unplug from the World Wide Web outside of work obligations. No cheating, no matter how strong the social media urge becomes.

-*Shop at small, local businesses.* Take a break from big supermarkets, department stores, and online shopping. Support your local deli, privately-owned convenience store, farm market, boutique, health food store, coop, or bakery.

-*Reserve time to not answer the phone.* Reserve an hour or chunk of time of *every day* to not be tied to a cell phone. If you usually feel like a switchboard operator, all the more reason to turn it off. Tell your contacts to text you in case of an emergency only.

-*Dedicate the week to healthier living.* Every day, do something good for your health, body, and psyche.

-*Don't watch television.* Tape your favorite shows and catch up with them another time. Use that extra time for something soul-nourishing.

-*Be completely yourself.* Dress, speak, think, act, and love authentically. There's nothing to prove, aspire to, come across as, or hide under a bushel for one week. Make your talents visible, laugh without restraint, be all that you are by being real.

-*Abandon perfectionism.* For seven days, don't strive for perfection and allow certain things to just *be.*

## Honoring Beauty

Making room for beauty in our lives should never be seen as superfluous, superficial, or reserved for those with financial ease. Beauty can be as simple as a sprig of goldenrod in a pretty vase or arranging strawberries artfully on a platter. Beauty, more than anything else, can make us stop in our tracks and breathe in the moment. Life is too short not to make a place for it in our daily routines. Seeing beauty makes us wealthy in the deepest way possible; it can be a gateway to healing, inspiration, and quality of life. Here are a few suggestions to fill your life with more beauty:

*-Make your bedside table an area of upliftment so the first thing you see every morning is something that inspires joy and inspiration.* You could include flowers, a photograph of a loved one or wonderful memory, and anything you hold precious. Dedicate it to the joys in life or your personal faith. Artfully arrange your treasures and memories, put down a special cloth, make sure it makes you smile.

*-Invite the seasons in.* Even places with temperate climates have their own subtlety of seasons, and each offers its own beauty. Find an area of your living space where you can celebrate and align with the turning of the year. String special-occasion lights over artificial greenery, flowers, or leaves according to season; add birds, seasonal books, framed photos or art, candles or aromatherapy diffusers, keepsakes from seasons' past. You can even incorporate this seasonal concept in your bathroom to liven up daily routine. Surround yourself with scents associated with the seasons...warm spices, florals, green notes, citrus and other fruits. Drape some faux wisteria, grapes, or realistic crimson leaves over a curtain rod.

-*Wear and surround yourself with beautiful colors.* Even if you work in a corporate setting, bringing color into your day can be as simple as choosing a piece of jewelry with a colorful stone or a tie with a spot of red. Get a brightly-colored throw pillow for the couch or new sheets in a color that makes your heart dance. Buy a special dish or bowl for your use only. Eating breakfast out of something beautiful and colorful can't help but start your day with a snippet of beauty.

-*Eat with beautiful music.* Put on music that brings peace and joy into your surroundings while you eat. Turn off the television, refuse to dwell on unsolved problems, and make it a time of nourishment on all levels. Do this even in the morning before you start your day.

-*Acknowledge beauty everywhere.* Take *notice* of clouds, wayside blooms, tufts of blowing grass, gold lights at twilight, the iridescent colors of pigeons, urban rhythms, sundown over a freeway, dew on early morning lawns, the first few stars, moths dancing around a light, the sound of children at play, a ray of sunlight in your beloved's hair, shapes of pebbles under your feet, reflections in a parking lot puddle. Make it a point to see the extraordinary in the ordinary.

-*Give credit where credit's due.* If you admire someone's coloring, dress, or talent, tell the person. It could make someone's day, or better, help them to see the beautiful and the good in themselves. See beauty and pass it on.

-*Take beauty breaks.* Spare two to five minutes to concentrate on something beautiful—in your surroundings, imagination, or memory. See it, feel it, take it into yourself for nourishment. It can be as small as taking note of a ring on your hand flashing colors in the light near a window.

-*See something beautiful in something you dislike.* If you hate rainy days, find something you like about them...the sensation of mist on your face or the sound of rain as you fall asleep. Practice seeing something good in the uninviting and uninspiring; it could change your perspective in ways you might not anticipate. Apply this with people, too.

-*Feel beautiful.* Feeling beautiful has nothing to do with gender and outward appearances. Feeling beautiful means responding to beauty—in all its forms and taking it into our psyches. Living a beautiful life doesn't take a lot of money, a lot of time, or fine taste, only an open heart.

# 8

# ℳ Nourished Life

## The Banquet Within

Despite modern self-containment for many of us, as humans, we need each other to survive on this planet. It is human to need assistance in various forms, depending upon our circumstances and physical-emotional-spiritual requirements. Sometimes we need a guiding hand, a seasoned mentor, a professional opinion, a loving friend, and other outside sources for advice, help, or just plain inspiration. It is also human to overly rely on these sources, for we tend to forget or mistrust our own internal knowledge and provisions.

If we cut through the distractions and noise of everyday living, it is possible to find the banquet of our own be-ing. This inner plenty is interwoven with our souls' indestructible life force and independent of anything outside of it that is for our lesser good. Sustenance of our own Divine Will, intuition, and spiritual connection does not come with a price and provides nourishment for a lifetime if we dare to trust it.

There is much false nourishment along our paths. Sometimes we grasp onto trends of enlightenment, self-help movements, and nutrition and diet fads and end up questioning things more than ever. Failing to see that we are each individual, we are susceptible to wanting the once-and-for-all answer and may burn out after we feel we have exhausted everything. We may even believe we have found The Way, finally, but live that particular way long enough to know that even the most profound answer only opens new questions, new journeys. The self is ever-changing, and that is a good thing. When our philosophies and beliefs morph into new uncertainty and epiphany, it is a great sign that we are growing.

The Self, on the other hand, is the ever-fixed light to the self (the shadow), the place we usually turn to last for answers. It is the succulent banquet that offers genuine satiety. The Self is beyond all that we perceive and is the ultimate, unchanging Truth. Aligning with the Self is simply allowing the path to sometimes find us, rather than the other way around; the feast finds our hunger when we raise our standards and only allow true nourishment (versus pseudo sustenance) to come into play.

We are born with deep wisdom and bubbling joy; babies and young children laugh easily, delight in the humblest of things, notice details of wondrous beauty, and commune with the outside world with an open heart. It takes very little for the young self to be satiated because our formative years are intricately linked to the Self, the Source. As we grow, we are molded by expectation, cultural views, and familial habit; little by little, the inner banquet is replaced with tempting illusions of happiness. We forget the bounty at the core of our beings yet long for something we cannot put our finger on, something that cannot be retrieved through the usual means.

## Identifying Poisons

The more we value ourselves, the more we are likely to make decisions that support our wellbeing. The more we get accustomed to putting our higher good into the daily equation, chances are that we will fine tune the ability to listen to our bodies and souls and come to know how to nourish both without a price.

There are many poisons to wellbeing—and poisons, like many other things in life—vary highly from individual to individual. Toxins come in many forms: the wrong diet, draining and challenging people, trying to make ill-fitting relationships work, placating whims of society, and putting ourselves last, just to name a few. The more honest we are with ourselves, the more we are able to cultivate spiritual discernment; the more we value the core Self, the stronger we become to make sometimes very difficult decisions that support a more contented life with peace at the center.

Things, activities, places, and people we love can be toxic to us, and there are a million inherited reasons why we maintain a close relationship to these poisons. Obligation. Being a 'good' person. Love. Blood ties. Emotional addiction. Vulnerability. Financial impotence. Each of us can experience any or all of these throughout a lifetime. Bottom line is that in the quest to "do the right thing," we might not do what's right for us. Loyalty to Shoulds and Have-Tos is part of being a responsible adult, but when that loyalty evolves to self-made prisons, our evolution is hindered. Identifying our individual poisons does not always have to lead to elimination of them, rather honing simple discernment about how much time, energy, and our life force we give to them. Sometimes just *knowing* our poisons can help us find what we need most for happier, healthier lives. Knowledge is power; self-knowledge is priceless.

We all can benefit by taking inventory of our toxins— in diet, living environment, work place, attitudes and emotions, relationships and people. Some of the relationships and things we love most can be toxic to our wellbeing and admitting this can cause distress or guilt, but there is no right or wrong, just self-honesty.

## The Role of Food

Nourishment on the physical level provides a found- ation for sustenance on every other and deserves more serious consideration. We fill our cars with premium gasoline for optimum performance, fortify our plants and gardens, and give our pets the best on the market yet find it laborious to feed our own bodies with care.

If we can safely consume a whole apple, arsenic-containing seeds and all, yet become ill if we eat only the seeds without the flesh of the fruit, what does this tell us? Nature provides everything in its whole state and when we meddle with this totality through processing, we compromise nutritional value as well as life force. As an example, today it is common to see fruit flavoring in foods rather than the actual thing. Companies, in the quest for cutting costs, have conditioned our taste buds to settle for mere flavor without the promise of nourishment. Conventional growing methods that incorporate chemicals rob nutrients from our food, and by the time it reaches our bellies, most of the inherent vitamins and minerals have been depleted along with flavor. The apples of organic wild trees, another example, are heady with aroma and luscious in flavor, a far cry from the rock-hard, waxed, bland and scentless "Snow White" apples at the supermarket. In essence, we have stripped nature from the actual harvest, and this violation is backfiring, most evident in our skyrocketing health epidemics.

Our relationship with food, like our human relation-ships, should also include respect if not reverence, joy, spiritual connection, and attention. Thankfully, many of us reading this have food on the table; therefore, we have a rare choice in how we relate to it. I think shifting our perspective to a healthier, more mindful one honors the blessing of bounty.

Taste, along with our other senses, has become jaded, and we need more and more of something to respond. Many of us have lost the ability to detect nuances of what we put in our mouths—subtlety of flavor, texture, and sweetness—and to make up for this, need the jolt of heavily spiced, salted, and sweetened foods to feel satisfied, however briefly. The enjoyment of food is severely lacking, which in turn, makes us reach for chemically-based flavors bearing little resemblance to the real thing. Our kids are growing into adulthood nutrient-deprived and addicted to imitations.

If we put long-term good health at the top of the list for what we want for the next generation instead of "getting them everything" we might see a dramatic change in how our kids feel physically and emotionally, how they learn in school, and how they feel about themselves. In essence, what could be more important? For them and for this world?

## A Time to Nourish...

Nourishment is a serious topic, but nourishing our bodies doesn't have to be serious. Going to the market can feel like a chore, but if we approach it with enthusiasm and our senses engaged, it can be a whole new experience of re-discovering the beauty of food.

### Try it for a week...

-If you are usually a consumer of white sugar, try switching to healthier sweeteners for a week: raw honey, organic dehydrated cane juice, agave nectar, stevia. If you are already well acquainted with alternative sweeteners, go off all sugars for a week.

-If you usually purchase pre-packaged salad greens, try buying whole head lettuces and preparing your own mixture.

-If you skip breakfast, try eating something in the morning. If you are already a breakfast eater, incorporate healthy foods you might not have tried yet: flaxseeds, whole grain steel-cut oats, organic eggs, alternative milks such as almond, rice, coconut, soy, or hemp.

-Really taste your food, every bite, every meal. Turn off the television, shut down the computer, and turn off your phone. Just *be* with your food.

-Pick a recipe you have time for and prepare it for yourself and a loved one.

-Don't eat fast food or packaged foods for a week and try to ride out your cravings.

-Try healthier salts such as Himalayan pink or Celtic gray.

-Use a crock pot and come home to a wonderful meal.

### Try it for a month...

-Reserve Sundays for an old-fashioned supper and invite someone special over or get together with friends for a potluck Sunday supper.

-Eat more foods in their raw state including nuts, veges, fruits; shred beets, carrots, turnips, zucchini, and apples into your salad; make some juice and ditch the pasteurized bottled variety.

-Go to the library and pick out ethnic cookbooks and get acquainted with cuisines from around the world. Pick a new recipe every week to try.

-Choose a traditional prayer or write your own to say before eating, every meal. It can be as simples as, "I am grateful for this bounty."

-Try slicing your veges on an angle, placing your food artfully on the plate (whatever looks pretty and appealing), drinking water from an elegant glass, eating with chopsticks, and garnishing with freshly-chopped herbs.

-Play uplifting music while you prepare a meal.

-Bake or cook a meal with your kids instead of going to the mall. Choose a healthy treat to make, put on some great music, and have some fun.

-Have weekly picnics, even if it's in your own living room on a rainy day.

-Eat by candlelight every evening.

-Try a new grain every week. A few suggestions: amaranth, teff, quinoa, buckwheat (kasha), millet.

-Slow down while you eat; chew well; nourishing our bodies shouldn't be a race against the clock.

## Feeding the Soul

Being mindful of our body's nourishment without making provision for the spirit is not living a nourished life. Many of us may go the extreme of eating well and working out regularly but fail to allow room for stillness, rest, joy, and recharging our spiritual batteries. The human being is not just the body but consciousness that accommodates the physical, emotional, mental, and spiritual planes. As long as one self is not being adequately sustained, our lives will continue to fall short of contented.

## Try it for a week...

-Do something daily, no matter how small, that makes you feel good and uplifted.

-Lessen the chasm between yourself and the natural world. Take a walk; take a drive to the country; have lunch in the park; walk your dog; picnic; press leaves into a book; find an interesting stone to put on your desk; choose your favorite animal or bird and get books from the library to learn more about it; listen to the rain or watch the snow fall while doing nothing else; look for feathers in the grass; watch the clouds; listen to the birds in the morning; sit by a body of water.

-Dedicate a day to a loved one who has passed. Eat their favorite food; remember good times; write them a letter; go to a place they enjoyed; call someone who also knew them and reminisce.

-Dedicate a day to pleasing your senses. Take a scented bath, invigorating shower or swim; smell a garden; wear feel-good fabrics; listen to music you love; eat something delightful. Don't wait for a day off; do it even on a work day. Enjoy your morning or evening bathing time. Play music in the car. Pack your own gourmet lunch.

-Start and end the day with something inspirational— a prayer, a song, a mantra, or affirmation.

-Revisit a childhood activity. Crayons, skipping rope, writing in a diary, dipping cookies into milk, reading a favorite story. Be a kid again for a little while.

-Find things you love about your life, right here, right now.

-Skip watching the news or reading the newspaper.

-Change a habit. Choose something that is not contributing to your wellbeing and drop it for seven days.

**Try it for a month...**

-Watch only happy, funny, or inspiring programs on television. Mute the commercials.

-Avoid trying to figure it all out. Forget the meaning of life, worrying about so-and-so, or obsessing over details. Take life *as is*, just for now.

-Do something creative, even if it's just doodling on a pad while talking on the phone. Cook. Buy fresh flowers and arrange them in a vase or bowl. Add more color into your life. Sing out loud and off key on your way to work.

-Keep your desk uncluttered.

-Choose someone inspirational to help you stick to a

healthier or more creative lifestyle...an ancestor, teacher, friend, Renaissance painter, poet, or spiritual teacher. Keep something in your environment to remind you of them- a quote, a framed image, or keepsake.

-Get more rest...physically, mentally, and emotionally. Find the invisible Off button inside and use it. Practice makes it easier.

-Refuse to participate in the drama of others, including loved ones. Also refuse to give in to your own.

-Play. With your kids, partner, pet. Dare to be goofy and leave room for silliness.

-Make soulful love, be in the moment. Love without boundaries.

-Read a page from one of your favorite books every night before going to sleep.

-Try to remember your dreams in the morning.

-Thank a loved one every day for something they did.

-Thank your body for trying its best and taking you through life, no matter how compromised your health may be.

-Replace bad memories immediately with good ones, even if it involves the same set of characters.

# 9
# B.L.I.S.S.

## Defining Bliss

Each of us is a multiplicity of preferences, emotions, and memories, unique unto ourselves. What brings me joy may not be the same for my friend or husband. We each have our own definition of bliss, and sometimes it changes with our age, consciousness, and circumstances in life.

What is *bliss* to you? What was bliss to you at age twenty? Thirty? Forty? What is bliss to you at this very moment?

For many of us, bliss is an elusive word and concept. We may have an idea of what we think it is or may have touched upon it at some time in our lives, but it remains nebulous when we attempt to reach out and grasp a definitive edge. I believe it is easier when we ask ourselves, "What emotion do we equate with bliss?" Joy? Excitement? Passion? Hope? Love? Self-confidence or containment? Achievement? Peace? Spiritual communion? Being true to our human nature, our answers will change from day to day, and to me, that is beautiful because it reminds me of how many options for bliss we all have.

For me, bliss is five simple nourishments: **B**eauty, **L**ove, **I**nspiration, **S**elf, and **S**pirit. B.L.I.S.S. These five nourishments can also be seen as tools, and we can take our toolbox anywhere.

## <u>Beauty</u>

Making room for beauty, as we have touched upon, is essential in experiencing the ecstatic or blissful. Making a commitment to seeing, honoring, and being surrounded by beauty engages our senses and feeds the soul. Without beauty, we are moved by little, and life is a continuous gray tunnel with no highs or lows. Beauty is our best friend on this human journey and the Higher Power in each of us beckons us to submerge ourselves in it.

Here are a few ways you can make a commitment to beauty:

-Make a beauty journal. It can be a simple pad of paper or a decorated diary, a place where you add something daily that you have noticed in your travels or felt emotionally or spiritually; a place where your deepest and most sacred observations of beauty will be recorded. You can simply write three words or pages describing your encounters with beauty, add photos, drawings, or mementos.

-Dedicate part of every day to noticing what is beautiful to your eye...the flower growing in the sidewalk, the color of a loved one's eyes in the sunlight, the intricate layers of seeds inside a kiwi. You name it...it's beautiful and you are the beholder.

-Collect quotes about beauty. Keep one or two near your desk or bedside and re-read them daily.

-Engage all of your senses in the observation of beauty. Taste beauty. Feel beauty. Hear beauty. See beauty. Smell beauty.

-Share the beauty you find…if you took a beautiful picture, share it with other people. If you see a rainbow or a sunset that stopped you in your tracks, tell a loved one or complete stranger. Experience beauty and then be an instrument of beauty by passing it on to others. Beauty is infectious as bad news…let's opt for the positive.

-Remain close to nature and find beauty there first when you feel you have run out of joy.

### Love

Love as emotion can bring us the greatest bliss or deepest pain; love as energy can bring healing at the core level. Throughout time, the thread that runs through most religions is the concept of love. All love is equal and divine when it is pure. Contrary to human understanding of love as emotion, in essence, love is energy. Energy is what we call God. God is love; we are energy; we are love. When we surrender ego and fear we can become like reeds in the wind and allow love to pass through us. It is then we can create with this energy and even manifest miracles.

During our modern challenging times, each of us must become spiritual warriors and individually invoke the power of love in our lives. Each person is a ripple on the surface of the pond that begets another. Perhaps, this is the nucleus of all religious or mystical quests: to reach a state of love, and then all else is possible. But to accomplish this, all doubt and fear must first be conquered or the pristine consciousness of love will be diluted.

Allotting room for love in our lives is also critical for living more blissfully. This does not mean we need to be in love, have a partner, or be a parent; it also does not mean we need others in order to align with the energy of love. Love is the free-flowing life force of the universe and independent of human ties and emotion. Love is pure essence of the Eternal within us.

Here is a meditation exercise you may wish to try or use regularly to feed your heart center, the place where the Self resides within the self. Perhaps you would like to do this with a friend, each taking turns to read the text aloud as a guide.

## Meditation for Living through the Heart

To begin, place your power hand (the hand you write with) over the area between your breastbone and where you feel your heartbeat. Take the time to feel your heartbeat beneath your fingertips. As you feel the silent, incessant drumming, think of someone you love, a beautiful memory, or your love for a Higher Power. If you have a favorite childhood memory, remember it in detail. If any memory is your object of focus, recall it with feeling. Return to that distant day and relive each moment that brings you warmth and joy. If you choose to think about someone you love, remember the person's laughter, smile, or voice. If you focus on a lover or spouse, remember his or her eyes lit with sunlight, a whispered touch, or a dissolving embrace. If you think of your longing and reverence for a Higher Power, remember that the glory of this Infinite Energy resides within the center your hand is resting on. Feel the invisible thread of light that connects you to this power like glimmering gossamer.

Once you feel submerged in your object of focus, begin to breathe deeply and evenly for a few long moments. Feel the breath reach all the way into your diaphragm, filling you with serenity and warmth. Feel your thoughts of a Higher Power, a lover, or a memory enter your body through your breath. Pretend you are not breathing air but the love that occupies your thoughts. If you have difficulty visualizing this, remember the smells of that lost day in your memory, the scent of your lover's clothes, or the sweetness of a house of worship.

When you feel that your mind and breathing are somewhat entwined (the more your thoughts and feelings are united, the better) think of the most beautiful rose color you have ever seen. Think of blushing, light-infused clouds hovering in an illumined dawn. Imagine deep pink roses lit with sun, undressing their glowing petals in a gust of morning wind. Feel the flower's silken clusters between your fingers. In your mind's eye, smell the fragrance of these glowing roses that resemble wine and rain. Envision rose-colored goblets overflowing with sunlight on a windowsill. Completely drench your mind with rose pink until all other thoughts are eclipsed by its fire. Allow the memory, the lover, the Higher Power to dissolve in the color of rose. Imagine this color in the palm of your hand that is resting on your chest. Visualize its pink fire blazing like a star and penetrating your heart. Continue to imagine this transference of light energy until you feel warmth inside your heart. This warmth will probably progress into a sensation of expansion, as if suddenly a door in your heart has flung open widely and your breathing feels weightless, even exhilarated. Once you reach this point, drop your power hand to your side and surrender entirely to the new sensations. Focus your mind on three things only:

*your breathing<br>
*the chair, floor, or bed against your back<br>
*the feeling in your heart

Focus only on these three things. If other thoughts interfere, allow them to pass and strive to channel all of your concentration into the above three objects of focus. Once you do this, drop one of the three. Now forget your breathing and only think of the bed or floor against your back and the feeling in your heart center. Again, focus only on these two things.

Now, drop another object of focus, the bed or floor against your back, and concentrate only on the feeling in your heart. If you get off track, again think of two things. Once you are able to singularly focus on the feeling in your heart, you may feel inseparable from the heart center itself. You should experience a loss of self and a profound communion with the present moment, the consciousness of Now. You *are* the heart. You *are* love. You *are* the rose, the energy, the power. You are your complete and untouchable *Self*.

Remain in this state for as long as you wish and then gradually come back to your everyday life, taking deep and relaxed breaths, holding the love inside yourself.

## Inspiration

Inspiration...Walt Whitman found it in the wilds; Jim Morrison found it on a rooftop on a California beach; Maya Angelou finds it in a hotel room stripped of all distractions and a bottle of sherry. What inspires you? And what are you inspired to do?

In the ancient world, inspiration was believed to be the great gift of the muses, supernatural beings who whispered in the ears of poets, artists, and philosophers. Always portrayed as female, muses would be called upon when venturing into artistic or visionary projects. Our words *music, museum,* and others come from the word muse; today, we can see the Muse as the wellspring of the Self, the inexhaustible source of energy from which ideas are born. The poet Garcia Lorca saw the creative process broken into a trinity: the muse (gives form), the angel (gives grace and light) and the *duende* (gives life). *Duende* is a component that varies in translation but always suggests deep pain or conflict that births greatness, a dark undertow beneath a wave catching the sunlight in its spindrift.

On this human journey, very few of us ever feel the apex of bliss without a riptide, the dark surge of pain beneath the crest. This is where the concept of *duende* can play a vital role in living our lives to the fullest. It is easy to rejoice ecstatically when everything is flowing in the direction of our intentions and hopes, but the challenge is to draw the ecstatic from the painful, times when even a glimmer of hope is absent. All great creators know this dichotomy, and we each can learn something valuable from them— perhaps, even, the most valuable lesson about cultivating bliss in our lives. We do not need to be artists or poets to be inspired, but as humans, we all need inspiration.

Many of us struggle through our silent hells without putting the pain to good use, and in turn, ascend to a higher state of resolution or tolerance. Using the creative spirit inside of us can be a tremendous tool to experiencing more bliss. Here are a few things you might like to try:

-Choose something in your present life or the past that is unresolved; choose something emotional that circles your consciousness in need of healing. Next, imagine this emotion as a color or set of colors. What colors would this conflict be? Take crayons, markers, or paints and use your colors depicting this emotional unrest. Apply them without any goal in mind; this is not about imitating Picasso or Van Gogh, only manifesting pain on paper. Use your fingers, handprint, whatever you are moved to do. Don't analyze it; just feel it. This is your moment to bring darkness into light, to birth what is beyond words into something tangible. Do as many as you like. There is no need to show anyone unless you want a kindred spirit to witness your manifestation. Make this a regular exercise. Keep your manifestations in a safe and sacred place or hang them somewhere to gather strength and resolve.

-In the same fashion as above, clip images from magazines and form a collage that depicts your emotional landscape.

-Begin a diary based only upon three words a day. This is a great exercise in distilling your experiences into essence. Three words. Every day. Nothing wasted, only the truth of your journey through life.

-Throw the ingredients for cookies into a bowl—from scratch or from a box. Immerse your hands in grains from the earth; imagine the wheat or the rice growing and blowing in the wind; imagine human hands gathering the crops and grinding them into flour. Feel the earth and be moved by this connection. In the ancient world, Ceres was considered to be the goddess responsible for grain, the embodiment of nourishment. Make your own connection between the earth and your belly's nourishment. Create sustenance.

-Gather flowers, leaves, and grasses during a challenging day and press them into a book. Retrieve them a week later and paste them to a lovely piece of art paper and frame them. Make something beautiful from what is not.

-When feeling overwhelmed by emotion, begin to move your body. Dance to anger, pain, grief, whatever you are going through. Let your emotions be your music urging you to free them from your body. In the philosophy of ecstatic dancer Gabrielle Roth, "Sweat your prayers."

-When you are in distress and find yourself pleading with a Higher Power for assistance, take a moment to create your own special prayer. Speak from your heart, shape something beautiful in the darkness.

-Do each or any of the above inspirational activities when you are also feeling joyful.

## <u>S</u>elf

Self, both the lower and upper case, is the essence of our personal life journeys. We are here to unite the self with the Self, to evolve the self into Self, to express Self as self. This simple knowledge can affect our decision-making, outlook and philosophy, goals, how we take care of ourselves and how we love. It is the most important tool in the B.L.I.S.S. toolbox, one that everything else hinges upon. Here are a few ideas to help remind you of your own value:

-Each morning, look into the mirror and say out loud or silently, "You are valuable. You are gifted. You matter. You can count on me to take care of you."

-Check in with yourself as you would someone you love. Tune into how you're feeling physically, emotionally, and spiritually.

-Thank your heart for beating, your brain for functioning and governing your body, your hands for serving you, your senses for their gifts, anything and everything your body does daily (no days off) to enable your survival.

## **Spirit**

Spirit can be defined in many ways; find what it means to you personally. Your outlook. Your soul-consciousness. Your passions. Your unique gifts and qualities. Your philosophy or approach to life. Your energy and positivity. Honoring your spirit is critical in finding and maintaining contentment; without it, everything else in life may seem meaningless. Here are a few ways to remain connected with your spirit, even on challenging and busy days:

-Feed your dream. Your dream can be a goal, a talent, a project, a plan, an idea, anything that puts wind in your sails when you think of it. Don't worry if it seems impossible to accomplish at the moment. Honor it with your thoughts and feelings, keep it alive with enthusiasm and good intention. Abandon excuses. Your dream does not want to hear them and has no concept of them. Keep it important and in your heart.

-Find a Higher Power to lean upon, even if it's your

great-grandmother who raised ten kids and never lost her faith in the face of hardship; even if it is your own will to survive and thrive; even if it's the ancient wisdom of the natural world. Find it, name it, and keep it close.

-Plan something to look forward to each day. It can be as simple as saying a prayer, listening to your favorite music, or making a smoothie that will rock your taste buds.

-Fill your life and consciousness with love. Surround yourself with things you love, people who love you, and anything that lifts your spirit daily. Love creates a circle of light, a barrier that keeps the negative from eating away at our potential for contentment.

### A Corner of Bliss

Inviting bliss into our lives can be as simple as making a Bliss Corner. A Bliss Corner can be a small portion of wall in your bedroom, office, or workspace where you place anything and everything that makes you truly happy when you look at it. Photos of good memories, loved ones, or inspirational art. Letters or keepsakes. Ticket stubs. A snippet of cloth that holds memories. Childhood keepsakes. Your kids' baby shoes. Photos of yourself you feel proud of. You get the idea.

The best place for a Bliss Corner is near the door of any room. This way, you can see it every time you enter or leave the space. Have fun and be creative...make your wall a mosaic of joy.

# Closing

## Joy Without a Reason

Our times are particularly challenging as we experience the side effects of progress, but I truly believe our spiritual evolution lies within nature's subtle wisdom: bloom where we are planted; fly even when broken-hearted; find joy despite imperfect circumstances. Like children, we too can laugh, love, and live inside the storm if we remember that joy for its own sake is reason enough to be joyful.

It is easier to find contentment when we matter to ourselves *enough* to shift our perspective, allow for our highest good to come to us, to re-evaluate our requirements for happiness. Contentment wants to find us as much as we need to find it.

Much like Rumi's "lovers don't just find each other somewhere; they are in each other all along," I close with the wondrous possibility and the question: What if the jewel of happiness is already in our possession, simply beneath the clutter?

I wish you all things beautiful. Be free!

# Bibliography

Beck, Deva. *Pleasure Connection: How Endorphins Affect Our Health and Happiness*. –Synthesis Press, 1987.

Davis, Albert H. *Something to Offend Everyone.*— 1991.

Druhan, Marlene Marie. *Naked Soul: Astral Travel and Cosmic Relationships.* St. Paul, MN: Llewellyn Publications, 1998.

Graham, Martha. *Blood Memory: An Autobiography.* New York, New York: Doubleday, 1991.

Hirsch, Edward. *The Demon and the Angel: Searching for the Source of Artistic Inspiration*. Boston, MA: HarCourt Books, 2003.

Riordan, James. *Break on Through: The Life and Death of Jim Morrison.* Medford, New Jersey: Plexus Publishing, 1991.

Roth, Gabrielle. *Sweat Your Prayers.* New York, New

York: Tarcher, 1998.

Rumi, Jalal al-Din. Barks, Coleman and Moyne, John (translation) *The Essential Rumi.* New York, New York: HarperOne, 2004.

Worwood, Valerie Ann. The Fragrant Mind: Aromatherapy for Personality, Mind, Mood, and Emotion. Novato, California. New World Library.

# Index

# About the Author

Marlaina Donato is the author of several books including the metaphysical title **Naked Soul** (Llewellyn, 1998) and the novel **Broken Jar**. She is also a multimedia artist. She and her beloved husband Joe and their canine muse live in beautiful rural New Jersey. To learn more about her books or to peruse her online visual art galleries, please visit: www.booksandbrush.net

www.ingramcontent.com/pod-product-compliance
Lightning Source LLC
Chambersburg PA
CBHW051829040426

42447CB00006B/443